FREEDOM OF THE PRESS DECISIONS OF THE UNITED STATES SUPREME COURT

MAUREEN HARRISON & STEVE GILBERT
EDITORS

FIRST AMENDMENT DECISIONS SERIES

EXCELLENT BOOKS
SAN DIEGO, CALIFORNIA

EXCELLENT BOOKS
Post Office Box 927105
San Diego, CA 92192-7105

Publisher's Cataloging in Publication Data

Freedom of the Press Decisions of the United States Supreme Court/
  Maureen Harrison, Steve Gilbert, editors.
    p. cm. - (First Amendment Decisions Series)
Bibliography: p.
Includes Index.
1. Freedom of the Press - United States - Cases.
2. Press law - United States. 3. United States. Supreme Court.
I. Title. II. Harrison, Maureen. III. Gilbert, Steve.
IV. Series: First Amendment Decisions.

KF4774.H24 1996   LC 96-83103
323.4-dc20

ISBN 1-880780-10-0

INTRODUCTION

The loss of liberty in general would soon follow the supression of the liberty of the press; for as it is an essential branch of liberty, so perhaps it is the best preservation of the whole. **- The New York Weekly Journal**
November 19, 1733

On November 17, 1734 John Peter Zenger, publisher of the New York *Weekly Journal*, was imprisoned for criticizing New York's Colonial Governor William Cosby. Zenger was defended by Philadelphia's Andrew Hamilton (no relation to Alexander) who, on August 4, 1734, summed up Zenger's case to the jury in this way: "The question before the Court and you gentlemen of the jury is not of small nor private concern, it is not the cause of a poor printer, nor of New York alone, which you are now trying: No! It may in its consequence affect every freeman that lives under a British government on the main of America. It is the best cause. It is the cause of liberty; and I make no doubt but your upright conduct this day will have laid a noble foundation for securing to ourselves, our posterity, and our neighbors that to which nature and the laws of our country have given us a right - the liberty - both of exposing and opposing arbitrary power by speaking and writing the truth." Zenger was acquitted.

A generation later the lessons of Zenger's imprisonment and trial for "speaking and writing the truth" were still on the minds of the Founding Fathers as they drafted the Constitution's First Amendment:

Thomas Jefferson: *Our liberty depends on the freedom of the press, and that cannot be limited without being lost.*

James Madison: *A popular Government, without popular information, or the means of acquiring it, is but a Prologue to a Farce or a Tragedy; or perhaps both. Knowledge will forever govern ignorance: And a people who mean to be their own Governors, must arm themselves with the power knowledge gives.*

Benjamin Franklin: *The Liberty of the Press: A liberty which every Pennsylvanian would fight and die for.*

The thirteen words that make up the First Amendment's Free Speech and Free Press Clauses

> *Congress shall make no law abridging freedom of speech or of the press*

are the Founding Father's guarantee, now in its 205th year, that Americans will have a right to a press free of Federal Government interference. The Constitution's Fourteenth Amendment, ratified in 1868, applies these same First Amendment protections against interference by state and local governments. The final arbiter of the meaning of the First Amendment's Free Speech and Free Press Clauses, given this role by the Constitution, is the United States Supreme Court.

In *Freedom Of The Press Decisions*, we have selected and edited fourteen First Amendment Free Press cases that clearly illustrate the importance that Jefferson, Madison, and Franklin put on the the legal battle - in the truest sense, the "war of words" - between the right of the press to freely publish and the power of the Government to interfere and punish.

Judge Learned Hand wrote: "The language of the law must not be foreign to the ears of those who are to obey it." The fourteen *Freedom Of The Press Decisions* presented in this book are carefully edited versions of the official texts issued by the Supreme Court in *United States Reports.* We, as editors, have made every effort to replace esoteric legalese with plain English without damaging the original decisions. Edited out are long alpha-numeric legal citations and wordy wrangles over points of procedure. Edited in are definitions (*writ of habeas corpus* = an order from a judge to bring a person to court), translations (*certiorari* = the decision of the Court to review a case), identifications (Appellant = The New York Times, Appellee = The United States Government), and explanations (where the case originated, how it got to the court, what the issues were, and who the parties were).

You will find in this book the majority opinion of the Court as expressed by the Justice chosen to speak for the Court. Preceding each edited decision, we note where the complete decision can be found. The bibliography provides a list of further readings on the cases and the Court. Also included for the reader's reference is a complete copy of the United States Constitution, to which every decision refers.

Every year over five thousand requests for review of lower court decisions are received by the Court. Requests, called petitions for *certiorari*, come to the Court from the losing side in Federal Appeals or State Supreme Courts. Four of the nine Justices must agree to a review. Only four hundred cases are accepted each year. Once accepted, written arguments, called briefs, pro and con, are submitted to the Court by both the petitioner, the side appealing the lower court decision against them, and the respondent, the side defending the lower court decision in their favor. Interested parties, called *amici curiae* [friends of the Court], may be permitted to file their own briefs in support of either side. After briefs are submitted to and reviewed by the Justices, public oral arguments are heard by the Court. Lawyers for the petitioner and respondent are allowed thirty minutes to make their case before the Justices. The Justices, at their discretion, may interrupt at any time to require further explanations, to pose hypothetical questions, or make observations.

Twice a week, on Wednesday and Friday, the Justices meet alone in conference to discuss each case and to vote on the outcome. They may affirm [uphold] or reverse [change the outcome of], in whole or in part, the decisions of the lower courts from which these appeals have come. One Justice, voting in the majority, will be selected to write the majority opinion. In rare instances the Court will issue its decision *per curiam* [by the Court majority without attribution of authorship]. Justices may join in the majority opinion, write their own concurring opinion, write their own dissenting opinion, or join in another's concurrence or dissent. Drafts of the majority, concurring, and dissenting opinions circulate among the Justices for their comments. Opinions are redrafted and recirculated until a consensus is reached and a carefully worded decision is announced. It is the majority decision that stands as the law of the land.

Justice William O. Douglas wrote this of the people who in 1791 authored the First Amendment:

> *The Framers of the Constitution knew human nature as well as we do. They too had lived in dangerous days; they too knew the suffocating influence of orthodoxy and standardized thought. They weighed the compulsions for restrained speech and thought against the abuses of liberty. They chose liberty.*

The representative selection of Supreme Court cases you will find in *Freedom Of The Press Decisions* is in its individual particulars about the rights and responsibilities of a free press in an open society.

In their broadest sense they are about "choosing liberty."

M.H. & S.G.

TABLE OF CONTENTS

Excluding The Press
143

A trial courtroom is a public place where the people generally - and representatives of the media - have a right to be present, and where their presence historically has been thought to enhance the integrity and quality of what takes place.

Chief Justice Warren Burger
Richmond Newspapers v. Virginia

Searches and Seizures In Newsrooms
163

The general submission is that searches of newspaper offices for evidence of crime reasonably believed to be on the premises will seriously threaten the ability of the press to gather, analyze, and disseminate news.

Justice Byron White
Zurcher v. Stanford Daily

X-Rated Cable Broadcasts
173

Patently offensive material from cable television stations can confront the citizen in the privacy of their home with little or no prior warning.

Justice Stephen Breyer
Denver Telecommunications v. FCC

The U.S. Constitution
193

*This book is dedicated to our friend and mentor
Glen T. Nygreen*

*In the First Amendment the Founding Fathers gave the
free press the protection it must have to fulfill its essential role in our democracy. The press was to serve the governed, not the governors. The Government's power to censor the press was abolished so that the press would remain
forever free to censure the Government. The press was
protected so that it could bare the secrets of government
and inform the people.*

- Justice Hugo Black

Malicious and Scandalous Newspapers
Near v. Minnesota

[Any person engaged in publishing] a malicious, scandalous and defamatory newspaper is guilty of a nuisance and may be permanently enjoined from publishing.
- Minnesota's 1925 Newspaper "Gag Law"

In 1925 the Minnesota Legislature enacted a Newspaper "Gag Law." This law made the publication of any "malicious, scandalous and defamatory" newspaper articles a public nuisance. A newspaper found guilty of publishing "malicious, scandalous and defamatory" articles was to be suppressed and its owners forbidden, under prior restraint, to ever publish any similar newspaper again.

The *Saturday Press*, a scandal sheet, was published by Jay Near in Minneapolis, Minnesota. In 1927 the Hennepin County Attorney brought a complaint against Near's *Saturday Press*, stating that its September through November editions were "largely devoted to malicious, scandalous and defamatory articles." The offending articles made criminal accusations against three public officials - Minneapolis' Mayor, Police Chief, and County Attorney - as well as anti-Semitic remarks about "Jewish gangsters."

The *Saturday Press* was found by the Hennepin County District Court to be a public nuisance and was suppressed. Near was forbidden to publish any similar kind of newspaper ever again. Claiming that the suppression of his newspaper and the prohibition of his right to publish was a violation of the First Amendment's Free Press Clause, Near appealed to the Minnesota Supreme Court, which unanimously upheld the constitutionality of the "Gag Law." Near appealed to the United States Supreme Court.

Oral arguments were heard on January 30, 1931 and on June 1, 1931 the 5-4 decision of the Court was announced by Chief Justice Charles Evans Hughes.

THE NEAR COURT

Chief Justice Charles Evans Hughes
Appointed Chief Justice by President Hoover
Served 1930 - 1941

Associate Justice Oliver Wendell Holmes, Jr.
Appointed by President Theodore Roosevelt
Served 1902 - 1932

Associate Justice Willis Van Devanter
Appointed by President Taft
Served 1910 - 1937

Associate Justice James McReynolds
Appointed by President Wilson
Served 1914 - 1941

Associate Justice Louis Brandeis
Appointed by President Wilson
Served 1916 - 1939

Associate Justice George Sutherland
Appointed by President Harding
Served 1922 - 1938

Associate Justice Pierce Butler
Appointed by President Harding
Served 1922 - 1939

Associate Justice Harlan Fiske Stone
Appointed by President Coolidge
Served 1925 - 1946

Associate Justice Owen Roberts
Appointed by President Hoover
Served 1930 -1945

The unedited text of *Near v. Minnesota* can be found on page 697, volume 283 of *United States Reports*.

NEAR v. MINNESOTA
June 1, 1931

CHIEF JUSTICE HUGHES: Chapter 285 of the Session Laws of Minnesota for the year 1925 provides for the abatement, as a public nuisance, of a "malicious, scandalous and defamatory newspaper, magazine or other periodical." Section one of the act is as follows:

"Section 1: Any person who, as an individual, or as a member or employee of a firm, or association or organization, or as an officer, director, member or employee of a corporation, shall be engaged in the business of regularly or customarily producing, publishing or circulating, having in possession, selling or giving away,

(a) an obscene, lewd and lascivious newspaper, magazine, or other periodical, or

(b) a malicious, scandalous and defamatory newspaper, magazine or other periodical,

is guilty of a nuisance, and all persons guilty of such nuisance may be enjoined [stopped] as hereinafter provided.

"Participation in such business shall constitute a commission of such nuisance and render the participant liable and subject to the proceedings, orders and judgments provided for in this act. Ownership, in whole or in part, directly or indirectly, of any such periodical, or of any stock or interest in any corporation or organization which owns the same in whole or in part, or which publishes the same, shall constitute such participation.

"In actions brought under (b) above, there shall be available the defense that the truth was published with good motives and for justifiable ends and in such actions the plaintiff [the person bringing the case to the court] shall not have the right to report [sic] to issues or editions of periodicals taking place more than three months before the commencement of the action."

. . . . Under this statute, (section one, clause (b)), the county attorney of Hennepin county brought this action to enjoin the publication of what was described as a "malicious, scandalous and defamatory newspaper, magazine and periodical," known as "The Saturday Press," published by [Near] in the city of Minneapolis. The complaint alleged that [Near] on September 24, 1927, and on eight subsequent dates in October and November, 1927, published and circulated editions of that periodical which were "largely devoted to malicious, scandalous and defamatory articles" concerning Charles G. Davis, Frank W. Brunskill, the Minneapolis Tribune, the Minneapolis Journal, Melvin C. Passolt, George E. Leach, the Jewish Race, [and] the members of the grand jury of Hennepin county impaneled in November, 1927. . . . While the complaint did not so allege, it appears . . . that Charles G. Davis was a special law enforcement officer employed by a civic organization, that George E. Leach was mayor of Minneapolis, that Frank W. Brunskill was its chief of police, and that Floyd B. Olson . . . was county attorney.

.... [T]he articles charged in substance that a Jewish gangster was in control of gambling, bootlegging and racketeering in Minneapolis, and that law enforcing officers and agencies were not energetically performing their duties. Most of the charges were directed against the chief of police; he was charged with gross neglect of duty, illicit relations with gangsters, and with participation in graft. The county attorney was charged with knowing the existing conditions and with failure to take adequate measures to remedy them. The mayor was accused of inefficiency and dereliction. One member of the grand jury was stated to be in sympathy with the gangsters. A special grand jury and a special prosecutor were demanded to deal with the situation in general, and, in particular, to investigate an attempt to assassinate one Guilford, one of the original defendants, who, it appears from the articles, was shot by gangsters after the first issue of the periodical had been published. There is no question but that the articles made serious accusations against the public officers named and others in connection with the prevalence of crimes and the failure to expose and punish them.

.... [O]n November 22, 1927, ... an order was made directing the defendants [Near] to show cause why a temporary injunction [court order stopping an action] should not issue and meanwhile forbidding the defendants to publish, circulate or have in their possession any editions of the periodical from September 24, 1927, to November 19, 1927, inclusive, and from publishing, circulating, or having in their possession, "any future editions of said The Saturday Press" and "any publication, known by any other name whatsoever containing malicious, scandalous and defamatory matter of the kind alleged." ...

[T]he Supreme Court (of Minnesota) sustained [let stand] the statute.... [D]efendant Near ... averred [confirmed] that he was the sole owner and proprietor of the publication in question. He admitted the publication of the articles in the issues described in the complaint but denied that they were malicious, scandalous or defamatory as alleged. He expressly invoked the protection of the due process clause of the 14th Amendment. . . . [Minnesota] moved that the court direct the issue of a permanent injunction, and this was done.

The district court . . . found . . . that the editions in question were "chiefly devoted to malicious, scandalous and defamatory articles," concerning the individuals named. The court further found that [Near] through these publications "did engage in the business of regularly and customarily producing, publishing and circulating a malicious, scandalous and defamatory newspaper," and that "the said publication" "under said name of The Saturday Press, or any other name, constitutes a public nuisance under the laws of the state." Judgment was thereupon entered adjudging that "the newspaper, magazine and periodical known as The Saturday Press, as a public nuisance, "be and is hereby abated." The judgment perpetually enjoined the defendants "from producing, editing, publishing, circulating, having in their possession, selling or giving away any publication whatsoever which is a malicious, scandalous or defamatory newspaper, as defined by law," and also "from further conducting said nuisance under the name and title of said The Saturday Press or any other name or title."

The defendant Near appealed from this judgment to the supreme court of the state, again asserting his right under the Federal Constitution, and the judgment was affirmed [upheld]. . . . The court added that it saw no reason "for [Near] to construe [interpret] the judgment as restraining [him] from operating a newspaper in harmony with the public welfare, to which all must yield." . . .

This statute, for the suppression as a public nuisance of a newspaper or periodical, is unusual, if not unique, and raises questions of grave importance transcending the local interests involved in the particular action. It is no longer open to doubt that the liberty of the press and of speech is within the liberty safeguarded by the due process clause of the 14th Amendment from invasion by state action. It was found impossible to conclude that this essential personal liberty of the citizen was left unprotected by the general guaranty of fundamental rights of person and property. In maintaining this guaranty, the authority of the State to enact laws to promote the health, safety, morals and general welfare of its people is necessarily admitted. . . . Liberty of speech and of the press is also not an absolute right, and the state may punish its abuse. Liberty, in each of its phases, has its history and connotation and, in the present instance, the inquiry is as to the historic conception of the liberty of the press and whether the statute under review violates the essential attributes of that liberty.

. . . . It is thus important to note precisely the purpose and effect of the statute as the state court has construed it.

First. The statute is not aimed at the redress of individual or private wrongs. Remedies for libel remain available and unaffected. The statute, said the state court, "is not directed at threatened libel but at an existing business which, generally speaking, involves more than libel." It is aimed at the distribution of scandalous matter as "detrimental to public morals and to the general welfare," tending "to disturb the peace of the community" and "to provoke assaults and the commission of crime." In order to obtain an injunction to suppress the future publication of the newspaper or periodical, it is not necessary to prove the falsity of the charges that have been made in the publication condemned. In the present action there was no allegation that the matter published was not true. It is alleged, and the statute requires the allegation, that the publication was "malicious." But, as in prosecutions for libel, there is no requirement of proof by the state of malice in fact as distinguished from malice inferred from the mere publication of the defamatory matter. The judgment in this case proceeded upon the mere proof of publication. The statute permits the defense, not of the truth alone, but only that the truth was published with good motives and for justifiable ends. It is apparent that under the statute the publication is to be regarded as defamatory if it injures reputation, and that it is scandalous if it circulates charges of reprehensible conduct, whether criminal or otherwise, and the publication is thus deemed to invite public reprobation and to constitute a public scandal. The court sharply defined the purpose of the statute, bringing out the precise point, in these words:

"There is no constitutional right to publish a fact merely because it is true. It is a matter of common knowledge that prosecutions under the criminal libel statutes do not result in efficient repression or suppression of the evils of scandal. Men who are the victims of such assaults seldom resort to the courts. This is especially true if their sins are exposed and the only question relates to whether it was done with good motives and for justifiable ends. This law is not for the protection of the person attacked nor to punish the wrongdoer. It is for the protection of the public welfare."

Second. The statute is directed not simply at the circulation of scandalous and defamatory statements with regard to private citizens, but at the continued publication by newspapers and periodicals of charges against public officers of corruption, malfeasance in office, or serious neglect of duty. Such charges by their very nature create a public scandal. They are scandalous and defamatory within the meaning of the statute, which has its normal operation in relation to publications dealing prominently and chiefly with the alleged derelictions of public officers.

Third. The object of the statute is not punishment, in the ordinary sense, but suppression of the offending newspaper or periodical. . . . It is the continued publication of scandalous and defamatory matter that constitutes the business and the declared nuisance. In the case of public officers, it is the reiteration of charges of official misconduct, and the fact that the newspaper or periodical is principally devoted to that purpose, that exposes it to suppression. In the present instance, the proof was that nine editions of the newspaper or periodical in question were published on successive dates, and that they were chiefly devoted to charges against public officers and in relation to the prevalence and protection of crime. In such a case, these officers are not left to their ordinary remedy in a suit for libel, or the authorities to a prosecution for criminal libel. Under this statute, a publisher of a newspaper or periodical, undertaking to conduct a campaign to expose and to censure official derelictions, and devoting his publication principally to that purpose, must face not simply the possibility of a verdict against him in a suit or prosecution for libel, but a determination that his newspaper or periodical is a public nuisance to be abated, and that this abatement and suppression will follow unless he is prepared with legal evidence to prove the truth of the charges and also to satisfy the court that, in addition to being true, the matter was published with good motives and for justifiable ends.

This suppression is accomplished by enjoining [stopping] publication and that restraint is the object and effect of the statute.

Fourth. The statute not only operates to suppress the offending newspaper or periodical but to put the publisher under an effective censorship. When a newspaper or periodical is found to be "malicious, scandalous and defamatory," and is suppressed as such, resumption of publication is punishable as a contempt of court by fine or imprisonment. Thus, where a newspaper or periodical has been suppressed because of the circulation of charges against public officers of official misconduct, it would seem to be clear that the renewal of the publication of such charges would constitute a contempt and that the judgment would lay a permanent restraint upon the publisher, to escape which he must satisfy the court as to the character of a new publication. Whether he would be permitted again to publish matter deemed to be derogatory to the same or other public officers would depend upon the court's ruling. In the present [case] the judgment restrained the defendants from "publishing, circulating, having in their possession, selling or giving away any publication whatsoever which is a malicious, scandalous or defamatory newspaper, as defined by law." . . . [T]he manifest inference is that, at least with respect to a new publication directed against official misconduct, the defendant would be held, under penalty of punishment for contempt as provided in the statute, to a manner of publication which the court considered to be "usual and legitimate" and consistent with the public welfare.

. . . [T]he operation and effect of the statute in substance is that public authorities may bring the owner or publisher of a newspaper or periodical before a judge upon a charge of conducting a business of publishing scandalous and defamatory matter - in particular that the matter consists of charges against public officers of official dereliction - and unless the owner or publisher is able and disposed to bring competent evidence to satisfy the judge that the charges are true and are published with good motives and for justifiable ends, his newspaper or periodical is suppressed and further publication is made punishable as a contempt. This is of the essence of censorship.

The question is whether a statute authorizing such proceedings in restraint of publication is consistent with the conception of the liberty of the press as historically conceived and guaranteed. In determining the extent of the constitutional protection, it has been generally, if not universally, considered that it is the chief purpose of the guaranty to prevent previous restraints upon publication. The struggle in England, directed against the legislative power of the licenser, resulted in renunciation of the censorship of the press. The liberty deemed to be established was thus described by Blackstone:

"The liberty of the press is indeed essential to the nature of a free state; but this consists in laying no *previous* restraints upon publications, and not in freedom from censure for criminal matter

when published. Every freeman has an undoubted right to lay what sentiments he pleases before
the public; to forbid this, is to destroy the freedom of the press; but if he publishes what is improper, mischievous or illegal, he must take the
consequence of his own temerity."

The distinction was early pointed out between the extent
of the freedom with respect to censorship under our constitutional system and that enjoyed in England. Here, as
Madison said,

"The great and essential rights of the people are
secured against legislative as well as against executive ambition. They are secured, not by laws
paramount to prerogative, but by constitutions
paramount to laws. This security of the freedom
of the press requires that it should be exempt not
only from previous restraint by the executive, as
in Great Britain, but from legislative restraint
also."

. . . . The preliminary freedom extends as well to the false
as to the true; the subsequent punishment may extend as
well to the true as to the false. This was the law of criminal libel apart from statute in most cases, if not in all.

. . . . [I]t is recognized that punishment for the abuse of
the liberty accorded to the press is essential to the protection of the public, and that the common law rules that
subject the libeler to responsibility for the public offense,
as well as for the private injury, are not abolished by the
protection extended in our constitutions. The law of
criminal libel rests upon that secure foundation. . . . For
whatever wrong [Near] has committed or may commit, by

his publications, the state appropriately affords both public and private redress by its libel laws. . . .

The exceptional nature of its limitations places in a strong light the general conception that liberty of the press, historically considered and taken up by the Federal Constitution, has meant, principally, although not exclusively, immunity from previous restraints or censorship. The conception of the liberty of the press in this country had broadened with the exigencies of the colonial period and with the efforts to secure freedom from oppressive administration. That liberty was especially cherished for the immunity it afforded from previous restraint of the publication of censure of public officers and charges of official misconduct. . . . In the letter sent by the Continental Congress (October 26, 1774) to the Inhabitants of Quebec, referring to the "five great rights," it was said: "The last right we shall mention, regards the freedom of the press. The importance of this consists, besides the advancement of truth, science, morality, and arts in general, in its diffusion of liberal sentiments on the administration of government, its ready communication of thoughts between subjects, and its consequential promotion of union among them, whereby oppressive officers are shamed or intimidated, into more honorable and just modes of conducting affairs." Madison, who was the leading spirit in the preparation of the 1st Amendment of the Federal Constitution, thus described the practice and sentiment which led to the guaranties of liberty of the press in state constitutions:

"In every state, probably, in the Union, the press has exerted a freedom in canvassing the merits and measures of public men of every description which has not been confined to the strict limits of the common law. On this footing the freedom of the press has stood; on this footing it yet stands. . . . Some degree of abuse is inseparable from the proper use of everything, and in no instance is this more true than in that of the press. It has accordingly been decided by the practice of the states, that it is better to leave a few of its noxious branches to their luxuriant growth, than, by pruning them away, to injure the vigour of those yielding the proper fruits. And can the wisdom of this policy be doubted by any who reflect that to the press alone, chequered as it is with abuses, the world is indebted for all the triumphs which have been gained by reason and humanity over error and oppression; who reflect that to the same beneficent source the United States owe much of the lights which conducted them to the ranks of a free and independent nation, and which have improved their political system into a shape so auspicious to their happiness? Had 'Sedition Acts,' forbidding every publication that might bring the constituted agents into contempt or disrepute, or that might excite the hatred of the people against the authors of unjust or pernicious measures, been uniformly enforced against the press, might not the United States have been languishing at this day under the infirmities of a sickly Confederation? Might they not, possibly, be miserable colonies, groaning under a foreign yoke?"

The fact that for approximately one hundred and fifty years there has been almost an entire absence of attempts to impose previous restraints upon publications relating to the malfeasance of public officers is significant of the deep-seated conviction that such restraints would violate constitutional right. Public officers, whose character and conduct remain open to debate and free discussion in the press, find their remedies for false accusations in actions under libel laws providing for redress and punishment, and not in proceedings to restrain the publication of newspapers and periodicals. The general principle that the constitutional guaranty of the liberty of the press gives immunity from previous restraints has been approved in many decisions under the provision of state constitutions.

The importance of this immunity has not lessened. While reckless assaults upon public men, and efforts to bring obloquy upon those who are endeavoring faithfully to discharge official duties, exert a baleful influence and deserve the severest condemnation in public opinion, it cannot be said that this abuse is greater, and it is believed to be less, than that which characterized the period in which our institutions took shape. Meanwhile, the administration of government has become more complex, the opportunities for malfeasance and corruption have multiplied, crime has grown to most serious proportions, and the danger of its protection by unfaithful officials and of the impairment of the fundamental security of life and property by criminal alliances and official neglect, emphasizes the primary need of a vigilant and courageous press, especially in great cities. The fact that the liberty of the press may be abused by miscreant purveyors of scandal does not make any the less necessary the immunity of the press from previous restraint in dealing with official misconduct. Subsequent punishment for such abuses as may exist is the appropriate remedy, consistent with constitutional privilege.

In attempted justification of the statute, it is said that it deals not with publication per se, but with the "business" of publishing defamation. If, however, the publisher has a constitutional right to publish, without previous restraint, an edition of his newspaper charging official derelictions, it cannot be denied that he may publish subsequent editions for the same purpose. He does not lose his right by exercising it. If his right exists, it may be exercised in publishing nine editions, as in this case, as well as in one edition. If previous restraint is permissible, it may be imposed at once; indeed, the wrong may be as serious in one publication as in several. Characterizing the publication as a business, and the business as a nuisance, does not permit an invasion of the constitutional immunity against restraint. Similarly, it does not matter that the newspaper or periodical is found to be "largely" or "chiefly" devoted to the publication of such derelictions. If the publisher has a right, without previous restraint, to publish them, his right cannot be deemed to be dependent upon his publishing something else, more or less, with the matter to which objection is made.

. . . . The statute in question cannot be justified by reason of the fact that the publisher is permitted to show . . . that the matter published is true and is published with good motives and for justifiable ends. If such a statute, authorizing suppression and injunction on such a basis, is constitutionally valid, it would be equally permissible for the legislature to provide that at any time the publisher of any newspaper could be brought before a court . . . and required to produce proof of the truth of his publication, or of what he intended to publish, and of his motives, or stand enjoined. If this can be done, the legislature may provide machinery for determining in the complete exercise of its discretion what are justifiable ends and restrain publication accordingly. And it would be but a step to a complete system of censorship. The recognition of authority to impose previous restraint upon publication in order to protect the community against the circulation of charges of misconduct, and especially of official misconduct, necessarily would carry with it the admission of the authority of the censor against which the constitutional barrier was erected. The preliminary freedom, by virtue of the very reason for its existence, does not depend, as this court has said, on proof of truth.

Equally unavailing is the insistence that the statute is designed to prevent the circulation of scandal which tends to disturb the public peace and to provoke assaults and the commission of crime. Charges of reprehensible conduct, and in particular of official malfeasance, unquestionably create a public scandal, but the theory of the constitutional guaranty is that even a more serious public evil would be caused by authority to prevent publication. . . . There is nothing new in the fact that charges of reprehensible conduct may create resentment and the disposition to resort to violent means of redress, but this well-understood tendency did not alter the determination to protect the press against censorship and restraint upon publication. As was said in *New Yorker Staats-Zeitung v. Nolan,* "If the township may prevent the circulation of a newspaper for no reason other than that some of its inhabitants may violently disagree with it, and resent its circulation by resorting to physical violence, there is no limit to what may be prohibited." The danger of violent reactions becomes greater with effective organization of defiant groups resenting exposure, and if this consideration warranted legislative interference with the initial freedom of publication, the constitutional protection would be reduced to a mere form of words.

For these reasons we hold the statute, so far as it authorized the proceedings in this action under clause (b) of section one, to be an infringement of the liberty of the press guaranteed by the 14th Amendment. We should add that this decision rests upon the operation and effect of the statute, without regard to the question of the truth of the charges contained in the particular periodical. The fact that the public officers named in this case, and those associated with the charges of official dereliction, may be deemed to be impeccable, cannot affect the conclusion that the statute imposes an unconstitutional restraint upon publication.

Judgment reversed.

LIBEL

New York Times v. Sullivan

As the whole world knows by now, thousands of Southern Negro students are engaged in widespread non-violent demonstrations in positive affirmation of the right to live in human dignity as guaranteed by the U.S. Constitution and the Bill of Rights.

Heed Their Rising Voices

On March 29, 1960 The Committee to Defend Martin Luther King purchased a full-page advertisement in the *New York Times* entitled *Heed Their Rising Voices*.

In paragraphs three and six of *Heed Their Rising Voices*, the Montgomery Alabama Police were charged with the mistreatment of non-violent civil rights protesters and their leader, the Reverend Dr. Martin Luther King, Jr.

The daily circulation of the *New York Times* that day was about 650,000. 394 copies were sent to Alabama and, of those, 35 copies circulated in Montgomery County. One of those copies went to L.B. Sullivan, Montgomery, Alabama Commissioner of Public Affairs. Sullivan, who supervised the Montgomery Police, sued the *New York Times* for libel. Although not mentioned by name, Sullivan charged that paragraphs three and six of *Heed Their Rising Voices* contained falsehoods intended to injure his reputation. The *New York Times* answered that they were protected from charges of libel made by a public official under the First Amendment's guarantee of a free press.

A Montgomery County Circuit Court jury awarded Sullivan $500,000. The Alabama Supreme Court affirmed. The *Times* appealed to the United States Supreme Court.

Oral arguments commenced on January 6, 1964. On March 9, 1964 Justice William Brennan announced the 9-0 decision of the Court. The edited text follows.

THE SULLIVAN COURT

Chief Justice Earl Warren
Appointed by President Eisenhower
Served 1953 - 1969

Associate Justice Hugo Black
Appointed by President Franklin Roosevelt
Served 1937 - 1971

Associate Justice William O. Douglas
Appointed by President Franklin Roosevelt
Served 1939 - 1975

Associate Justice Tom Clark
Appointed by President Truman
Served 1949 - 1967

Associate Justice John Marshall Harlan
Appointed by President Eisenhower
Served 1955 - 1971

Associate Justice William J. Brennan, Jr.
Appointed by President Eisenhower
Served 1956 - 1990

Associate Justice Potter Stewart
Appointed by President Eisenhower
Served 1958 - 1981

Associate Justice Byron White
Appointed by President Kennedy
Served 1962 - 1993

Associate Justice Arthur Goldberg
Appointed by President Kennedy
Served 1962 - 1965

The unedited text of *New York Times v. Sullivan* can be found on page 254, volume 376, of *United States Reports.*

NEW YORK TIMES v. SULLIVAN
March 9, 1964

JUSTICE BRENNAN: We are required in this case to determine for the first time the extent to which the constitutional protections for speech and press limit a State's power to award damages in a libel action [suit for publication of material injurious to one's reputation] brought by a public official against critics of his official conduct.

Respondent L.B. Sullivan is one of the three elected Commissioners of the City of Montgomery, Alabama. He testified that he was "Commissioner of Public Affairs and the duties are supervision of the Police Department and Fire Department. . . ." He brought this . . . libel action against petitioner . . . the *New York Times*, a daily newspaper. A jury in the Circuit Court of Montgomery County awarded him damages of $500,000, the full amount claimed, . . . and the Supreme Court of Alabama affirmed [upheld].

[Sullivan]'s complaint alleged that he had been libeled by statements in a full-page advertisement that was carried in the *New York Times* on March 29, 1960 entitled "Heed Their Rising Voices." The advertisement began by stating that "As the whole world knows by now, thousands of Southern Negro students are engaged in widespread non-violent demonstrations in positive affirmation of the right to live in human dignity as guaranteed by the U.S. Constitution and the Bill of Rights." It went on to charge that "in their efforts to uphold these guarantees, they are being met by an unprecedented wave of terror by those who would deny and negate that document which the whole world looks upon as setting the pattern for modern freedom. . . ." Succeeding paragraphs purported to illustrate the "wave of terror" by describing certain alleged events. The text concluded with an appeal for funds for three purposes; support of the student movement, "the struggle for the right-to-vote," and the legal defense of Dr. Martin Luther King, Jr., leader of the movement, against a perjury [lying under oath] indictment [charge] then pending in Montgomery.

. . . . The advertisement was signed at the bottom of the page by the "Committee to Defend Martin Luther King and the Struggle for Freedom in the South." . . .

Of the ten paragraphs of text in the advertisement, the third and a portion of the sixth were the basis of [Sullivan]'s claim of libel. They read as follows:

Third paragraph:

> "In Montgomery, Alabama, after students sang 'My Country, 'Tis of Thee' on the State Capitol steps, their leaders were expelled from school, and truckloads of police armed with shotguns and tear-gas ringed the Alabama State College Campus. When the entire student body protested to state authorities by refusing to re-register, their dining hall was padlocked in an attempt to starve them into submission."

Sixth paragraph:

> "Again and again the Southern violators have answered Dr. King's peaceful protests with intimidation and violence. They have bombed his home almost killing his wife and child. They have assaulted his person. They have arrested him seven

times - for 'speeding', 'loitering' and similar
'offenses.' And now they have charged him with
'perjury' - a *felony* [a crime of a serious nature]
under which they could imprison him for *ten
years.* . . ."

Although neither of these statements mentions [Sullivan]
by name, he contended that the word "police" in the third
paragraph referred to him as the Montgomery Commissioner who supervised the Police Department, so that he
was being accused of "ringing" the campus with police.
He further claimed that the paragraph would be read as
imputing to the police, and hence to him, the padlocking
of the dining hall in order to starve the students into submission. As to the sixth paragraph, he contended that
since arrests are ordinarily made by the police, the statement "They have arrested [Dr. King] seven times" would
be read as referring to him; he further contended that the
"They" who did the arresting would be equated with the
"They" who committed the other described acts and with
the "Southern violators." Thus, he argued, the paragraph
would be read as accusing the Montgomery police, and
hence him, of answering Dr. King's protests with
"intimidation and violence," bombing his home, assaulting
his person, and charging him with perjury. [Sullivan] and
six other Montgomery residents testified that they read
some or all of the statements as referring to him in his capacity as Commissioner.

It is uncontroverted that some of the statements contained
in the two paragraphs were not accurate descriptions of
events which occurred in Montgomery. Although Negro
students staged a demonstration on the State Capitol steps,
they sang the National Anthem and not "My Country, 'Tis
of Thee." Although nine students were expelled by the

State Board of Education, this was not for leading the demonstration at the Capitol, but for demanding service at a lunch counter in the Montgomery County Courthouse on another day. Not the entire student body, but most of it, had protested the expulsion, not by refusing to register, but by boycotting classes on a single day; virtually all the students did register for the ensuing semester. The campus dining hall was not padlocked on any occasion, and the only students who may have been barred from eating there were the few who had neither signed a preregistration application nor requested temporary meal tickets. Although the police were deployed near the campus in large numbers on three occasions, they did not at any time "ring" the campus, and they were not called to the campus in connection with the demonstration on the State Capitol steps, as the third paragraph implied. Dr. King had not been arrested seven times, but only four; and although he claimed to have been assaulted some years earlier in connection with his arrest for loitering outside a courtroom, one of the officers who made the arrest denied that there was such an assault.

On the premise that the charges in the sixth paragraph could be read as referring to him, [Sullivan] was allowed to prove that he had not participated in the events described. Although Dr. King's home had in fact been bombed twice when his wife and child were there, both of these occasions antedated [Sullivan]'s tenure as Commissioner, and the police were not only not implicated in the bombings, but had made every effort to apprehend those who were.

Three of Dr. King's four arrests took place before [Sullivan] became Commissioner. Although Dr. King had in fact been indicted (he was subsequently acquitted [found innocent]) on two counts of perjury, each of which carried a possible five-year sentence, [Sullivan] had nothing to do with procuring the indictment.

[Sullivan] made no effort to prove that he suffered actual pecuniary [monetary] loss as a result of the alleged libel. One of his witnesses, a former employer, testified that if he had believed the statements, he doubted whether he "would want to be associated with anybody who would be a party to such things that are stated in that ad," and that he would not re-employ [Sullivan] if he believed "that he allowed the Police Department to do the things that the paper says he did." But neither this witness nor any of the others testified that he had actually believed the statements in their supposed reference to [Sullivan].

. . . . The manager of the [*New York Times*] Advertising Acceptability Department testified that he had approved the advertisement for publication because he knew nothing to cause him to believe that anything in it was false, and because it bore the endorsement of "a number of people who are well known and whose reputation" he "had no reason to question." Neither he nor anyone else at the *Times* made an effort to confirm the accuracy of the advertisement, either by checking it against recent *Times* news stories relating to some of the described events or by any other means.

. . . . The *Times* did, however, subsequently publish a retraction of the advertisement upon the demand of Governor John Patterson of Alabama, who asserted that the publication charged him with "grave misconduct and . . . improper actions and omissions as Governor of Alabama and Ex-Officio Chairman of the State Board of Education of Alabama." When asked to explain why there had been a retraction for the Governor but not for [Sullivan], the Secretary of the *Times* testified: "We did that because we didn't want anything that was published by the *Times* to be a reflection on the State of Alabama and the Governor was, as far as we could see, the embodiment of the State of Alabama and the proper representative of the State and, furthermore, we had by that time learned more of the actual facts which the ad purported to recite and, finally, the ad did refer to the action of the State authorities and the Board of Education presumably of which the Governor is the ex-officio chairman. . . ." On the other hand, he testified that he did not think that "any of the language in there referred to Mr. Sullivan."

. . . . In affirming the judgment, the Supreme Court of Alabama sustained [maintained] the trial judge's rulings and . . . held that "where the words published tend to injure a person libeled by them in his reputation, profession, trade or business, or charge him with an indictable offense, or tend to bring the individual into public contempt," they are "libelous per se"; that "the matter complained of is, under the above doctrine, libelous per se, if it was published of and concerning the plaintiff"; and that it was actionable without "proof of pecuniary injury . . . , such injury being implied." It approved the trial court's ruling that the jury could find the statements to have been made "of and concerning" [Sullivan], stating: "We think it common knowledge that the average person knows that municipal agents, such as police and firemen, and others, are under the control and direction of the city governing body, and more particularly under the direction and control of a single commissioner. In measuring the performance or deficiencies of such groups, praise or criticism is usually attached to the official in complete control of the body." In sustaining the trial court's determination that the verdict was not excessive, the court said that malice could be inferred from the *Times'* "irresponsibility" in printing the advertisement while "the *Times* in its own files had articles already published which would have demonstrated the falsity of the allegations in the advertisement"; from the *Times'* failure to retract for [Sullivan] while retracting for the Governor, whereas the falsity of some of the allegations was then known to the *Times* and "the matter contained in the advertisement was equally false as to both parties"; and from the testimony of the *Times'* Secretary that, apart from the statement that the dining hall was padlocked, he thought the two paragraphs were "substantially correct." The court reaffirmed a statement in an earlier opinion that "There is no legal measure of damages in cases of this character." It rejected petitioners' constitutional contentions with the brief statements that "The First Amendment of the U.S. Constitution does not protect libelous publications" and "The Fourteenth Amendment is directed against State action and not private action."

Because of the importance of the constitutional issues involved, we [agreed to hear the case]. We reverse the judgment. We hold that the rule of law applied by the Alabama courts is constitutionally deficient for failure to provide the safeguards for freedom of speech and of the press that are required by the First and Fourteenth Amendments in a libel action brought by a public official against critics of his official conduct. We further hold that under the proper safeguards the evidence presented in this case is constitutionally insufficient to support the judgment for [Sullivan].

. . . . The publication here . . . communicated information, expressed opinion, recited grievances, protested claimed abuses, and sought financial support on behalf of a movement whose existence and objectives are matters of the highest public interest and concern. That the *Times* was paid for publishing the advertisement is as immaterial in this connection as is the fact that newspapers and books are sold. Any other conclusion would discourage newspapers from carrying "editorial advertisements" of this type, and so might shut off an important outlet for the promulgation of information and ideas by persons who do not themselves have access to publishing facilities - who wish to exercise their freedom of speech even though they are not members of the press. The effect would be to shackle the First Amendment in its attempt to secure "the widest possible dissemination of information from diverse and antagonistic sources." To avoid placing such a handicap upon the freedoms of expression, we hold that if the allegedly libelous statements would otherwise be constitutionally protected from the present judgment, they do not forfeit that protection because they were published in the form of a paid advertisement.

Under Alabama law as applied in this case, a publication is "libelous per se" if words "tend to injure a person . . . in his reputation" or to "bring [him] into public contempt"; the trial court stated that the standard was met if the words are such as to "injure him in his public office, or impute misconduct to him in his office, or want of official integrity, or want of fidelity to a public trust . . . ." The jury must find that the words were published "of and concerning" the plaintiff [a person who brings a case to the court], but where the plaintiff is a public official his place in the governmental hierarchy is sufficient evidence to support a finding that his reputation has been affected by statements that reflect upon the agency of which he is in charge. Once "libel per se" has been established, the defendant has no defense as to stated facts unless he can persuade the jury that they were true in all their particulars. His privilege of "fair comment" for expressions of opinion depends on the truth of the facts upon which the comment is based. . . .

The question before us is whether this rule of liability, as applied to an action brought by a public official against critics of his official conduct, abridges the freedom of speech and of the press that is guaranteed by the First and Fourteenth Amendments.

. . . . The general proposition that freedom of expression upon public questions is secured by the First Amendment has long been settled by our decisions. The constitutional safeguard, we have said, "was fashioned to assure unfettered interchange of ideas for the bringing about of political and social changes desired by the people. The maintenance of the opportunity for free political discussion to the end that government may be responsive to the will of the people and that changes may be obtained by lawful means, an opportunity essential to the security of the Republic, is a fundamental principle of our constitutional system." "[I]t is a prized American privilege to speak one's mind, although not always with perfect good taste, on all public institutions," and this opportunity is to be afforded for "vigorous advocacy" no less than "abstract discussion." The First Amendment, said Judge Learned Hand, "presupposes that right conclusions are more likely to be gathered out of a multitude of tongues, than through any kind of authoritative selection. To many this is, and always will be, folly; but we have staked upon it our all." Justice Brandeis, in his concurring opinion in *Whitney v. California*, gave the principle its classic formulation:

"Those who won our independence believed . . . that public discussion is a political duty; and that this should be a fundamental principle of the American government. They recognized the risks to which all human institutions are subject. But they knew that order cannot be secured merely through fear of punishment for its infraction; that it is hazardous to discourage thought, hope and imagination; that fear breeds repression; that repression breeds hate; that hate menaces stable government; that the path of safety lies in the opportunity to discuss freely supposed grievances and proposed remedies; and that the fitting remedy for evil counsels is good ones. Believing in the power of reason as applied through public discussion, they eschewed silence coerced by law - the argument of force in its worst form. Recognizing the occasional tyrannies of governing majorities, they amended the Constitution so that free speech and assembly should be guaranteed."

Thus we consider this case against the background of a profound national commitment to the principle that debate on public issues should be uninhibited, robust, and wide-open, and that it may well include vehement, caustic, and sometimes unpleasantly sharp attacks on government and public officials. The present advertisement, as an expression of grievance and protest on one of the major public issues of our time, would seem clearly to qualify for the constitutional protection. The question is whether it forfeits that protection by the falsity of some of its factual statements and by its alleged defamation of [Sullivan].

Authoritative interpretations of the First Amendment guarantees have consistently refused to recognize an exception for any test of truth - whether administered by judges, juries, or administrative officials - and especially one that puts the burden of proving truth on the speaker. The constitutional protection does not turn upon "the truth, popularity, or social utility of the ideas and beliefs which are offered." As Madison said, "Some degree of abuse is inseparable from the proper use of every thing; and in no instance is this more true than in that of the press." . . .

Allowance of the defense of truth, with the burden of proving it on the defendant, does not mean that only false speech will be deterred. Even courts accepting this defense as an adequate safeguard have recognized the difficulties of adducing [presenting] legal proofs that the alleged libel was true in all its factual particulars. Under such a rule, would-be critics of official conduct may be deterred from voicing their criticism, even though it is believed to be true and even though it is in fact true, because of doubt whether it can be proved in court or fear of the expense of having to do so. They tend to make only statements which "steer far wider of the unlawful zone." The rule thus dampens the vigor and limits the variety of public debate. It is inconsistent with the First and Fourteenth Amendments.

. . . . [W]e similarly conclude that the facts do not support a finding of actual malice. The statement by the *Times'* Secretary that, apart from the padlocking allegation, he thought the advertisement was "substantially correct," . . . affords no constitutional warrant for the Alabama Supreme Court's conclusion that it was a "cavalier ignoring of the falsity of the advertisement [from which]

the jury could not have but been impressed with the bad faith of the *Times*, and its maliciousness inferable therefrom." The statement does not indicate malice at the time of the publication; even if the advertisement was not "substantially correct" that opinion was at least a reasonable one, and there was no evidence to impeach the witness' good faith in holding it. The *Times'* failure to retract upon [Sullivan]'s demand, although it later retracted upon the demand of Governor Patterson, is likewise not adequate evidence of malice for constitutional purposes.
. . .

Finally, there is evidence that the *Times* published the advertisement without checking its accuracy against the news stories in the *Times'* own files. The mere presence of the stories in the files does not, of course, establish that the *Times* "knew" the advertisement was false, since the state of mind required for actual malice would have to be brought home to the persons in the *Times'* organization having responsibility for the publication of the advertisement. . . . We think the evidence against the *Times* supports at most a finding of negligence in failing to discover the misstatements, and is constitutionally insufficient to show the recklessness that is required for a finding of actual malice.

. . . . There was no reference to [Sullivan] in the advertisement, either by name or official position. A number of the allegedly libelous statements - the charges that the dining hall was padlocked and that Dr. King's home was bombed, his person assaulted, and a perjury prosecution instituted against him - did not even concern the police; despite the ingenuity of the arguments which would attach this significance to the word "They," it is plain that these statements could not reasonably be read as accusing

[Sullivan] of personal involvement in the acts in question.
. . .

The judgment of the Supreme Court of Alabama is reversed and the case is remanded to that court for further proceedings not inconsistent with this opinion.

The Pentagon Papers
New York Times v. United States

The essence of journalism is to make information available. How could we say to our readers: "We know, but you can't know?" - **A.M. Rosenthal, Managing Editor, The New York Times**

On June 13, 1971 the New York *Times* began to publish excerpts from the "History of U.S. Decision-Making Process on Viet Nam Policy," a "Top Secret" Defense Department study outlining in detail the history of the United States' involvement in the Viet Nam War. The Washington *Post* began to publish excerpts on June 18. This study had been illegally obtained by the newspapers from a former government official, Dr. Daniel Ellsberg, one of its authors. "The History of U.S. Decision-Making Process on Viet Nam Policy" become known as The Pentagon Papers.

The Justice Department under President Nixon's Attorney General John Mitchell attempted to obtain in the federal courts injunctions [court orders forbidding] further publication on national security grounds. New York's U.S. District Court refused, on First Amendment grounds, to issue an injunction against the *Times.* The U.S. Court of Appeals (Second Circuit) overturned that refusal. The *Times* appealed to the Supreme Court. Washington, D.C.'s U.S. District Court, also on First Amendment grounds, refused to issue an injunction against the *Post.* The U.S. Court of Appeals (District of Columbia Circuit) upheld this refusal. The Justice Department appealed to the Supreme Court.

The United States Supreme Court granted a review to both the New York *Times* and the Justice Department. Oral arguments were heard June 26 and on June 30, 1971 a brief 6-3 *Per Curiam* [by the Court] decision was announced, accompanied by six concurrences and three dissents.

THE PENTAGON PAPERS COURT

Chief Justice Warren Burger
Appointed Chief Justice by President Nixon
Served 1969 - 1986

Associate Justice Hugo Black
Appointed by President Franklin Roosevelt
Served 1937 - 1971

Associate Justice William O. Douglas
Appointed by President Franklin Roosevelt
Served 1939 - 1975

Associate Justice John Marshall Harlan
Appointed by President Eisenhower
Served 1955 - 1971

Associate Justice William Brennan
Appointed by President Eisenhower
Served 1956 -1990

Associate Justice Potter Stewart
Appointed by President Eisenhower
Served 1958 - 1981

Associate Justice Byron White
Appointed by President Kennedy
Served 1962 - 1993

Associate Justice Thurgood Marshall
Appointed by President Lyndon Johnson
Served 1967 - 1991

Associate Justice Harry Blackmun
Appointed by President Nixon
Served 1970 - 1994

The unedited text of *New York Times v. United States* can be found on page 713, volume 403 of *United States Reports.*

NEW YORK TIMES v. UNITED STATES
June 30, 1971

PER CURIAM [by the entire Court]: We granted certiorari [agreed to review] these cases in which the United States seeks to enjoin [stop] the New York Times and the Washington Post from publishing the contents of a classified study entitled "History of U.S. Decision-Making Process on Viet Nam Policy" [The Pentagon Papers].

"Any system of prior restraints of expression [stopping of publication] comes to this Court bearing a heavy presumption against its constitutional validity." The Government "thus carries a heavy burden of showing justification for the imposition of such a restraint." The District Court for the Southern District of New York in the *New York Times* case and the District Court ... and the Court of Appeals for the District of Columbia Circuit in the *Washington Post* case held that the Government had not met that burden. We agree.

The judgment of the Court of Appeals for the District of Columbia Circuit is therefore affirmed [upheld]. The order of the Court of Appeals for the Second circuit is reversed and the case is remanded [returned to the lower court for reruling].

JUSTICE HUGO BLACK, joined by JUSTICE WILLIAM DOUGLAS, concurring: I adhere to the view that the Government's case against the Washington *Post* should have been dismissed and that the injunction against the New York *Times* should have been vacated [cancelled] without oral argument when the cases were first presented to this Court. I believe that every moment's continuance of the injunctions against these newspapers amounts to a flagrant, indefensible, and continuing violation of the First Amendment. . . .

Our Government was launched in 1789 with the adoption of the Constitution. The Bill of Rights, including the First Amendment, followed in 1791. Now, for the first time in the one hundred and eight-two years since the founding of the Republic, the federal courts are asked to hold that the First Amendment does not mean what it says, but rather means that the Government can halt the publication of current news of vital importance to the people of this country.

In seeking injunctions against these newspapers and in its presentation to the Court, the Executive Branch seems to have forgotten the essential purpose and history of the First Amendment. When the Constitution was adopted, many people strongly opposed it because the document contained no Bill of Rights to safeguard certain basic freedoms. They especially feared that the new powers granted to a central government might be interpreted to permit the government to curtail freedom of religion, press, assembly, and speech. In response to an overwhelming public clamor, James Madison offered a series of amendments to satisfy citizens that these great liberties would remain safe and beyond the power of government to abridge. Madison proposed what later became the First Amendment in three parts, two of which are set out below, and one of which proclaimed: "The people shall not be deprived or abridged of their right to speak, to write, or to publish their sentiments; *and the freedom of the press, as one of the great bulwarks of liberty, shall be inviolable.*" The amendments were offered to *curtail* and *restrict* the general powers granted to the Executive, Legislative, and Judicial Branches two years before in the original Constitution. The Bill of Rights changed the original Constitution into a new charter under which no branch of government could abridge the people's freedoms of press, speech, religion, and assembly. Yet the Solicitor General [the Government's lawyer] argues . . . that the general powers of the Government adopted in the original Constitution should be interpreted to limit and restrict the specific and emphatic guarantees of the Bill of Rights adopted later. I can imagine no greater perversion of history. Madison and the other Framers of the First Amendment, able men that they were, wrote in language they earnestly believed could never be misunderstood: "Congress shall make no law . . . abridging the freedom . . of the press. . . ." Both the history and language of the First Amendment support the view that the press must be left free to publish news, whatever the source, without censorship, injunctions, or prior restraints.

In the First Amendment the Founding Fathers gave the free press the protection it must have to fulfill its essential role in our democracy. The press was to serve the governed, not the governors. The Government's power to censor the press was abolished so that the press would remain forever free to censure the Government. The press was protected so that it could bare the secrets of government and inform the people. Only a free and unrestrained press can effectively expose deception in government. And paramount among the responsibilities of a free press is the duty to prevent any part of the government from deceiving the people and sending them off to distant lands to die of foreign fevers and foreign shot and shell. In my view, far from deserving condemnation for their courageous reporting, the New York *Times*, the Washington *Post*, and other newspapers should be commended for serving the purpose that the Founding Fathers saw so clearly. In revealing the workings of government that led to the Vietnam war, the newspapers nobly did precisely that which the Founders hoped and trusted they would do.

. . . . [T]he Government argues . . . that in spite of the First Amendment, "[t]he authority of the Executive Department to protect the nation against publication of information whose disclosure would endanger the national security stems from two interrelated sources: the constitutional power of the President over the conduct of foreign affairs and his authority as Commander-in-Chief."

In other words, we are asked to hold that despite the First Amendment's emphatic command, the Executive Branch, the Congress, and the Judiciary can make laws enjoining publication of current news and abridging freedom of the press in the name of "national security." The Government does not even attempt to rely on any act of Congress. Instead it makes the bold and dangerously far-reaching contention that the courts should take it upon themselves to "make" a law abridging freedom of the press in the name of equity, presidential power and national security, even when the representatives of the people in Congress have adhered to the command of the First Amendment and refused to make such a law. To find that the President has "inherent power" to halt the publication of news by resort to the courts would wipe out the First Amendment and destroy the fundamental liberty and security of the very people the Government hopes to make "secure." No one can read the history of the adoption of the First Amendment without being convinced beyond any doubt that it was injunctions like those sought here that Madison and his collaborators intended to outlaw in this Nation for all time.

The word "security" is a broad, vague generality whose contours should not be invoked to abrogate [annul] the fundamental law embodied in the First Amendment. The guarding of military and diplomatic secrets at the expense of informed representative government provides no real security for our Republic. The Framers of the First Amendment, fully aware of both the need to defend a new nation and the abuses of the English and Colonial governments, sought to give this new society strength and security by providing that freedom of speech, press, religion, and assembly should not be abridged. This thought was eloquently expressed in 1937 by Chief Justice Hughes ... when the Court held a man could not be punished for attending a meeting run by Communists.

> "The greater the importance of safeguarding the community from incitements to the overthrow of our institutions by force and violence, the more imperative is the need to preserve inviolate the constitutional rights of free speech, free press and free assembly in order to maintain the opportunity for free political discussion, to the end that government may be responsive to the will of the people and that changes, if desired, may be obtained by peaceful means. Therein lies the security of the Republic, the very foundation of constitutional government."

The Rape Shield Law
Cox Broadcasting v. Cohn

It shall be unlawful for any news media to print, publish, broadcast or televise the name or identity of any female rape victim. - **Georgia's Rape Shield Law**

On August 18, 1971 a seventeen-year-old high school girl was raped and murdered by a gang of six in Sandy Springs, Georgia. Under Georgia's Rape Shield Law, enacted to insure the privacy of sexual assault victims, newspapers and televisions stations were prohibited from publishing or broadcasting her name. The trial of her accused rapists and murderers began on April 10, 1972. Tom Wassell, a reporter for a local television station WSB-TV, obtained, through public court records, the name of the victim: Cynthia Leslie Cohn. Wassell publicly broadcast her name over WSB-TV, despite Georgia's Rape Shield Law.

Martin Cohn, Cynthia's father, sued Cox Broadcasting, owner of WSB-TV, claiming that his right to privacy had been invaded. He claimed that WSB-TV's broadcast of his murdered daughter's name was in violation of her right to privacy under the Georgia Rape Shield Law.

Cox Broadcasting countered that they had, while covering a newsworthy event, obtained the victim's name from records open to the public and that the law prohibiting the broadcast of that name was in violation of their First Amendment Free Press Clause and Fourteenth Amendment Due Process Clause rights.

A Fulton County Court found for Martin Cohn, as did the Georgia Supreme Court. Cox Broadcasting appealed the verdict to the United States Supreme Court.

Oral arguments were heard on November 11, 1974 and the 8-1 decision of the Court was announced on March 3, 1975 by Associate Justice Byron White.

THE COX COURT

Chief Justice Warren Burger
Appointed Chief Justice by President Nixon
Served 1969 - 1986

Associate Justice William O. Douglas
Appointed by President Franklin Roosevelt
Served 1939 - 1975

Associate Justice William Brennan
Appointed by President Eisenhower
Served 1956 -1990

Associate Justice Potter Stewart
Appointed by President Eisenhower
Served 1958 - 1981

Associate Justice Byron White
Appointed by President Kennedy
Served 1962 - 1993

Associate Justice Thurgood Marshall
Appointed by President Lyndon Johnson
Served 1967 - 1991

Associate Justice Harry Blackmun
Appointed by President Nixon
Served 1970 - 1994

Associate Justice Lewis Powell
Appointed by President Nixon
Served 1971 - 1987

Associate Justice William Rehnquist
Appointed by President Nixon
Served 1971 -

The unedited text of *Cox Broadcasting v. Cohn* can be found on page 469, volume 420 of *United States Reports.*

COX BROADCASTING v. COHN
March 3, 1975

JUSTICE WHITE: The issue before us in this case is whether, consistently with the First and Fourteenth Amendments, a State may [sue] for damages for invasion of privacy caused by the publication of the name of a deceased rape victim which was publicly revealed in connection with the prosecution of the crime.

In August 1971, appellee [Cohn]'s seventeen-year-old daughter was the victim of a rape and did not survive the incident. Six youths were soon indicted for [charged with] murder and rape. Although there was substantial press coverage of the crime and of subsequent developments, the identity of the victim was not disclosed pending trial, perhaps because of [the Georgia law] which makes it a misdemeanor to publish or broadcast the name or identity of a rape victim. In April 1972, some eight months later, the six defendants appeared in court. Five pleaded guilty to rape or attempted rape, the charge of murder having been dropped. The guilty pleas were accepted by the court, and the trial of the defendant pleading not guilty was set for a later date.

In the course of the proceedings that day, appellant Wassell, a reporter covering the incident for his employer, learned the name of the victim from an examination of the indictments which were made available for his inspection in the courtroom. That the name of the victim appears in the indictments and that the indictments were public records available for inspection are not disputed. Later that day, Wassell broadcast over the facilities of station WSB-TV, a television station owned by appellant Cox Broadcasting Corp., a news report concerning the court proceedings. The report named the victim of the crime and was repeated the following day.

In May 1972, [Cohn sued Cox Broadcasting], . . . claiming that his right to privacy had been invaded by the television broadcasts giving the name of his deceased daughter. [Cox] admitted the broadcasts but claimed that they were privileged under both state law and the First and Fourteenth Amendments. The trial court, rejecting [Cox's] constitutional claims [found for Cohn]. . . .

On appeal, the Georgia Supreme Court . . . [stated that] whether the public discourse of the name actually invaded [Cohn]'s "zone of privacy," and if so, to what extent, were issues to be determined by the trier of fact [the jury]. Also, "in formulating such an issue for determination by the fact-finder, it is reasonable to require [Cohn] to prove that [Cox Broadcasting] invaded his privacy with wilful or negligent disregard for the fact that reasonable men would find the invasion highly offensive." . . .

Upon . . . rehearing the Georgia court countered the argument that the victim's name was a matter of public interest and could be published with impunity [stating that it was] state policy that the name of a rape victim was not a matter of public concern. This time the court felt compelled to determine the constitutionality of the statute and sustained [upheld] it as a "legitimate limitation on the right of freedom of expression contained in the First Amendment." The court could discern "no public interest or general concern about the identity of the victim of such a crime as will make the right to disclose the identity of the victim rise to the level of First Amendment protection."

. . . . We conclude that [we have] jurisdiction [authority] and reverse the judgment of the Georgia Supreme Court.

. . . . Since 1789, Congress has granted this Court appellate jurisdiction with respect to state litigation only after the highest state court in which judgment could be had has rendered a "[f]inal judgment or decree." . . .

Georgia stoutly defends [its statute regarding the privacy of a rape victim] challenged here. Its claims are not without force, for powerful arguments can be made, and have been made, that however it may be ultimately defined, there *is* a zone of privacy surrounding every individual, a zone within which the State may protect him from intrusion by the press, with all its attendant publicity. . . .

More compellingly, the century has experienced a strong tide running in favor of the so-called right of privacy. In 1967, we noted that "[i]t has been said that a 'right of privacy' has been recognized at common law in thirty States plus the District of Columbia and by statute in four States." . . . Nor is it irrelevant here that the right of privacy is no recent arrival in the jurisprudence of Georgia, which has embraced the right in some form since 1905 when the Georgia Supreme Court decided the leading case of *Pavesich v. New England Life Insurance Company.*

These are impressive credentials for a right of privacy, but we should recognize that we do not have at issue here an action for the invasion of privacy involving the appropriation of one's name or photograph, a physical or other tangible intrusion into a private area, or a publication of otherwise private information that is also false although perhaps not defamatory. The version of the privacy tort [legal wrong] now before us - termed in Georgia "the tort of public disclosure," is that in which the plaintiff [Cohn] claims the right to be free from unwanted publicity about his private affairs, which, although wholly true, would be offensive to a person of ordinary sensibilities. Because the gravamen [gist] of the claimed injury is the publication of information, whether true or not, the dissemination of which is embarrassing or otherwise painful to an individual, it is here that claims of privacy most directly confront the constitutional freedoms of speech and press. The face-off is apparent, and [Cox] urge[s] . . . that the press may not be made criminally or civilly liable for publishing information that is neither false nor misleading but absolutely accurate, however damaging it may be to reputation or individual sensibilities.

It is true that in defamation actions, where the protected interest is personal reputation, the prevailing view is that truth is a defense. . . .

The Court has nevertheless carefully left open the question whether the First and Fourteenth Amendments require that truth be recognized as a defense in a defamation action brought by a private person as distinguished from a public official or public figure. *Garrison* held that where criticism is of a public official and his conduct of public business, "the interest in private reputation is overborne by the larger public interest, secured by the Constitution, in the dissemination of truth," but recognized that "different interests may be involved where purely private libels, totally unrelated to public affairs, are concerned; therefore, nothing we say today is to be taken as intimating any views as to the impact of the constitutional guarantees in the discrete area of purely private libels." . . .

In this sphere of collision between claims of privacy and those of the free press, the interests on both sides are plainly rooted in the traditions and significant concerns of our society. Rather than address the broader question whether truthful publications may ever be subjected to civil or criminal liability consistently with the First and Fourteenth Amendments, or to put it another way, whether the State may ever define and protect an area of privacy free from unwanted publicity in the press, it is appropriate to focus on the narrower interface between press and privacy that this case presents, namely, whether the State may impose sanctions on the accurate publication of the name of a rape victim obtained from public records - more specifically, from judicial records which are maintained in connection with a public prosecution and which themselves are open to public inspection. We are convinced that the State may not do so.

In the first place, in a society in which each individual has but limited time and resources with which to observe at first hand the operations of his government, he relies necessarily upon the press to bring to him in convenient form the facts of those operations. Great responsibility is accordingly placed upon the news media to report fully and accurately the proceedings of government, and official records and documents open to the public are the basic data of governmental operations. Without the information provided by the press most of us and many of our representatives would be unable to vote intelligently or to register opinions on the administration of government generally. With respect to judicial proceedings in particular, the function of the press serves to guarantee the fairness of trials and to bring to bear the beneficial effects of public scrutiny upon the administration of justice.

[Cohn] has claimed in this litigation that the efforts of the press have infringed his right to privacy by broadcasting to the world the fact that his daughter was a rape victim. The commission of crime, prosecutions resulting from it, and judicial proceedings arising from the prosecutions, however, are without question events of legitimate concern to the public and consequently fall within the responsibility of the press to report the operations of government.

The special protected nature of accurate reports of judicial proceedings has repeatedly been recognized. This Court, in an opinion written by Justice Douglas, has said:

> "A trial is a public event. What transpires in the court room is public property. If a transcript of the court proceedings had been published, we suppose none would claim that the judge could punish the publisher for contempt. And we can see no difference though the conduct of the attorneys, of the jury, or even of the judge himself, may have reflected on the court. *Those who see and hear what transpired can report it with impunity.* There is no special perquisite of the judiciary which enables it, as distinguished from other institutions of democratic government, to suppress, edit, or censor events which transpire in proceedings before it."

. . . . [E]ven the prevailing law of invasion of privacy generally recognizes that the interests in privacy fade when the information involved already appears on the public record. The conclusion is compelling when viewed in terms of the First and Fourteenth Amendments and in light of the public interest in a vigorous press. The Geor-

gia [suit] for invasion of privacy through public disclosure of the name of a rape victim imposes sanctions on
pure expression - the content of a publication - and not
conduct or a combination of speech and nonspeech elements that might otherwise be open to regulation or prohibition. The publication of truthful information available on the public record contains none of the indicia of
those limited categories of expression, such as "fighting"
words, which "are no essential part of any exposition of
ideas, and are of such slight social value as a step to truth
that any benefit that may be derived from them is clearly
outweighed by the social interest in order and morality."

By placing the information in the public domain on official court records, the State must be presumed to have
concluded that the public interest was thereby being
served. Public records by their very nature are of interest
to those concerned with the administration of government,
and a public benefit is performed by the reporting of the
true contents of the records by the media. The freedom
of the press to publish that information appears to us to
be of critical importance to our type of government in
which the citizenry is the final judge of the proper conduct of public business. In preserving that form of government the First and Fourteenth Amendments command
nothing less than that the States may not impose sanctions
on the publication of truthful information contained in
official court records open to public inspection.

We are reluctant to embark on a course that would make
public records generally available to the media but forbid
their publication if offensive to the sensibilities of the
supposed reasonable man. Such a rule would make it very
difficult for the media to inform citizens about the public
business and yet stay within the law. The rule would in-

vite timidity and self-censorship and very likely lead to the suppression of many items that would otherwise be published and that should be made available to the public. At the very least, the First and Fourteenth Amendments will not allow exposing the press to liability for truthfully publishing information released to the public in official court records. If there are privacy interests to be protected in judicial proceedings, the States must respond by means which avoid public documentation or other exposure of private information. Their political institutions must weigh the interests in privacy with the interests of the public to know and of the press to publish. Once true information is disclosed in public court documents open to public inspection, the press cannot be sanctioned for publishing it. In this instance as in others reliance must rest upon the judgment of those who decide what to publish or broadcast.

[Wassell] based his televised report upon notes taken during the court proceedings and obtained the name of the victim from the indictments handed to him at his request during a recess in the hearing. [Cohn] has not contended that the name was obtained in an improper fashion or that it was not on an official court document open to public inspection. Under these circumstances, the protection of freedom of the press provided by the First and Fourteenth Amendments bars the State of Georgia from making [Cox's] broadcast the basis of civil liability.

Reversed.

The Infliction Of Emotional Distress
Hustler v. Falwell

[Hustler's parody, "Jerry Falwell Talks About His "First Time," was] the most hurtful, damaging, despicable, low-type personal attack that I can imagine one human being can inflict upon another. - **The Reverend Jerry Falwell**

Hustler Magazine published in its November 1983 issue a parody of a well-known liquor advertisement in which celebrities were interviewed about the "first time" they tried the product. The ad parody contained a supposed "interview" with the Reverend Jerry Falwell, a nationally known, politically active, Christian conservative minister. In the "interview," entitled "Jerry Falwell Talks About His First Time," the ad parody stated the Reverend's "first time" [a none too subtle double entendre about his first sexual experience] was during a drunken incestuous rendezvous with his mother in an outhouse. In small print at the bottom of the page was the disclaimer: "Ad parody - Not to be taken seriously." Reverend Falwell took the ad parody very seriously and brought legal action against *Hustler Magazine* and its publisher Larry Flynt, to recover damages for libel, invasion of privacy, and the intentional infliction of emotional distress. *Hustler* countered that their right to free expression under the First Amendment's Free Press Clause was absolute and ran the ad parody a second time.

In U.S. District Court a jury found *Hustler* guilty on one of the three charges, the intentional infliction of emotional distress, and awarded Falwell damages. *Hustler* appealed to the U.S. Court of Appeals, which affirmed the verdict. *Hustler* appealed to the United States Supreme Court.

Oral arguments were heard on December 2, 1987 and the 8-0 decision of the Court was announced on February 24, 1988 by Chief Justice William Rehnquist.

THE HUSTLER COURT

Chief Justice William Rehnquist
Appointed Chief Justice By President Reagan
Appointed Associate Justice by President Nixon
Served 1971 -

Associate Justice William Brennan
Appointed by President Eisenhower
Served 1956 -1990

Associate Justice Byron White
Appointed by President Kennedy
Served 1962 - 1993

Associate Justice Thurgood Marshall
Appointed by President Lyndon Johnson
Served 1967 - 1991

Associate Justice Harry Blackmun
Appointed by President Nixon
Served 1970 - 1994

Associate Justice John Paul Stevens
Appointed by President Ford
Served 1975 -

Associate Justice Sandra Day O'Connor
Appointed by President Reagan
Served 1981 -

Associate Justice Antonin Scalia
Appointed by President Reagan
Served 1986 -

Associate Justice Anthony Kennedy
Appointed by President Reagan
Served 1988 -

The unedited text of *Hustler Magazine v. Falwell* can be found on page 46, volume 485 of *United States Reports.*

HUSTLER MAGAZINE v. FALWELL
February 24, 1988

CHIEF JUSTICE WILLIAM REHNQUIST: Petitioner [Hustler Magazine] is a magazine of nation-wide circulation. Respondent [Jerry Falwell], a nationally known minister who has been active as a commentator on politics and public affairs, sued [Hustler and its publisher,] Larry Flynt, to recover damages for invasion of privacy, libel, and intentional infliction of emotional distress. The District Court directed a verdict against [Falwell] on the privacy claim, and submitted the other two claims to a jury. The jury found for [Hustler/Flynt] on the defamation claim, but found for [Falwell] on the claim for intentional infliction of emotional distress and awarded damages. We now consider whether this award is consistent with the First and Fourteenth Amendments of the United States Constitution.

The inside front cover of the November 1983 issue of Hustler Magazine featured a "parody" of an advertisement for Campari Liqueur that contained the name and picture of [Falwell] and was entitled "Jerry Falwell talks about his first time." This parody was modeled after actual Campari ads that included interviews with various celebrities about their "first times." Although it was apparent by the end of each interview that this meant the first time they sampled Campari, the ads clearly played on the sexual double entendre of the general subject of "first times." Copying the form and layout of these Campari ads, Hustler's editors chose [Falwell] as the featured celebrity and drafted an alleged "interview" with him in which he states that his "first time" was during a drunken incestuous rendezvous with his mother in an outhouse. The Hustler parody portrays [Falwell] and his mother as drunk and immoral, and suggests that [Falwell] is a hypocrite who preaches only when he is drunk. In small print at the bottom of the page, the ad contains the disclaimer, "ad parody - not to be taken seriously." The magazine's table of contents also lists the ad as "Fiction; Ad and Personality Parody."

Soon after the November issue of Hustler became available to the public, [Falwell] brought [suit] in the United States District Court for the Western District of Virginia against Hustler Magazine, Inc., Larry C. Flynt, and Flynt Distributing Co. [Falwell] stated in his complaint that publication of the ad parody in Hustler entitled him to recover damages for libel, invasion of privacy, and intentional infliction of emotional distress. The case proceeded to trial. At the close of the evidence, the District Court granted a directed verdict for [Hustler/Flynt] on the invasion of privacy claim. The jury then found against [Falwell] on the libel claim, specifically finding that the ad parody could not "reasonably be understood as describing actual facts about [Falwell] or actual events in which [he] participated." The jury ruled for [Falwell] on the intentional infliction of emotional distress claim, however, and stated that he should be awarded $100,000 in compensatory damages, as well as $50,000 each in punitive damages from [Hustler/Flynt]. . . .

On appeal, the United States Court of Appeals for the Fourth Circuit affirmed [upheld] the judgment against [Hustler/Flynt]. The court rejected [their] argument that the "actual malice" standard of *New York Times Co. v. Sullivan* must be met before [Falwell] can recover for emotional distress. The court agreed that because [Falwell] is concededly a public figure, [Hustler/Flynt] are "entitled to the same level of first amendment protection in the claim for intentional infliction of emotional distress that they received in [Falwell's] claim for libel." But this does not mean that a literal application of the actual malice rule is appropriate in the context of an emotional distress claim. In the court's view, the *New York Times* decision emphasized the constitutional importance not of the falsity of the statement or the defendant's disregard for the truth, but of the heightened level of culpability embodied in the requirement of "knowing . . . or reckless" conduct. Here, the *New York Times* standard is satisfied by the state-law requirement, and the jury's finding, that the defendants have acted intentionally or recklessly. The Court of Appeals then went on to reject the contention that because the jury found that the ad parody did not describe actual facts about [Falwell], the ad was an opinion that is protected by the First Amendment. As the court put it, this was "irrelevant," as the issue is "whether [the ad's] publication was sufficiently outrageous to constitute intentional infliction of emotional distress." [Hustler/Flynt] then filed a petition for rehearing [by the Court of Appeals], but this was denied by a divided court. Given the importance of the constitutional issues involved, we granted certiorari [agreed to review of the decision].

This case presents us with a novel question involving First Amendment limitations upon a State's authority to protect its citizens from the intentional infliction of emotional distress. We must decide whether a public figure may recover damages for emotional harm caused by the publication of an ad parody offensive to him, and doubtless gross and repugnant in the eyes of most.

[Falwell] would have us find that a State's interest in protecting public figures from emotional distress is sufficient to deny First Amendment protection to speech that is patently offensive and is intended to inflict emotional injury, even when that speech could not reasonably have been interpreted as stating actual facts about the public figure involved. This we decline to do.

At the heart of the First Amendment is the recognition of the fundamental importance of the free flow of ideas and opinions on matters of public interest and concern. "[T]he freedom to speak one's mind is not only an aspect of individual liberty - and thus a good unto itself - but also is essential to the common quest for truth and the vitality of society as a whole." We have therefore been particularly vigilant to ensure that individual expressions of ideas remain free from governmentally imposed sanctions. The First Amendment recognizes no such thing as a "false" idea. As Justice Holmes wrote, "[W]hen men have realized that time has upset many fighting faiths, they may come to believe even more than they believe the very foundations of their own conduct that the ultimate good desired is better reached by free trade in ideas - that the best test of truth is the power of the thought to get itself accepted in the competition of the market. . . ."

The sort of robust political debate encouraged by the First Amendment is bound to produce speech that is critical of those who hold public office or those public figures who are "intimately involved in the resolution of important public questions or, by reason of their fame, shape events in areas of concern to society at large." Justice Frankfurter put it succinctly in *Baumgartner v. United States*, when he said that "[o]ne of the prerogatives of American citizenship is the right to criticize public men and measures." Such criticism, inevitably, will not always be reasoned or moderate; public figures as well as public officials will be subject to "vehement, caustic, and sometimes unpleasantly sharp attacks." "[T]he candidate who vaunts his spotless record and sterling integrity cannot convincingly cry 'Foul!' when an opponent or an industrious reporter attempts to demonstrate the contrary."

Of course, this does not mean that *any* speech about a public figure is immune from sanction in the form of damages. Since *New York Times Co. v. Sullivan*, we have consistently ruled that a public figure may hold a speaker liable for the damage to reputation caused by publication of a defamatory falsehood, but only if the statement was made "with knowledge that it was false or with reckless disregard of whether it was false or not." False statements of fact are particularly valueless; they interfere with the truth-seeking function of the marketplace of ideas, and they cause damage to an individual's reputation that cannot easily be repaired by counterspeech, however persuasive or effective. But even though falsehoods have little value in and of themselves, they are "nevertheless inevitable in free debate," and a rule that would impose strict liability on a publisher for false factual assertions would have an undoubted "chilling" effect on speech relating to public figures that does have constitutional value. "Freedoms of expression require 'breathing space.'" This breathing space is provided by a constitutional rule that allows public figures to recover for libel or defamation only when they can prove *both* that the statement was false and that the statement was made with the requisite level of [blameworthiness].

[Falwell] argues, however, that a different standard should apply in this case because here the State seeks to prevent not reputational damage, but the severe emotional distress suffered by the person who is the subject of an offensive publication. In [Falwell]'s view, and in the view of the Court of Appeals, so long as the utterance was intended to inflict emotional distress, was outrageous, and did in fact inflict serious emotional distress, it is of no constitutional import whether the statement was a fact or an opinion, or whether it was true or false. . . . [T]he State's interest in preventing emotional harm simply outweighs whatever interest a speaker may have in speech of this type.

Generally speaking the law does not regard the intent to inflict emotional distress as one which should receive much solicitude, and it is quite understandable that most if not all jurisdictions have chosen to make it civilly culpable where the conduct in question is sufficiently "outrageous." But in the world of debate about public affairs, many things done with motives that are less than admirable are protected by the First Amendment. In *Garrison v. Louisiana*, we held that even when a speaker or writer is motivated by hatred or ill-will his expression was protected by the First Amendment:

> "Debate on public issues will not be uninhibited if the speaker must run the risk that it will be proved in court that he spoke out of hatred; even if he did speak out of hatred, utterances honestly believed contribute to the free interchange of ideas and the ascertainment of truth."

Thus while such a bad motive may be deemed controlling for purposes of . . . liability in other areas of the law, we think the First Amendment prohibits such a result in the area of public debate about public figures.

Were we to hold otherwise, there can be little doubt that political cartoonists and satirists would be subjected to damages awards without any showing that their work falsely defamed its subject. Webster's defines a caricature as "the deliberately distorted picturing or imitating of a person, literary style, etc. by exaggerating features or mannerisms for satirical effect." The appeal of the political cartoon or caricature is often based on exploration of unfortunate physical traits or politically embarrassing events - an exploration often calculated to injure the feelings of the subject of the portrayal. The art of the cartoonist is often not reasoned or evenhanded, but slashing and one-sided. One cartoonist expressed the nature of the art in these words:

> "The political cartoon is a weapon of attack, of scorn and ridicule and satire; it is least effective when it tries to pat some politician on the back. It is usually as welcome as a bee sting and is always controversial in some quarters."

Several famous examples of this type of intentionally injurious speech were drawn by Thomas Nast, probably the greatest American cartoonist to date, who was associated for many years during the post-Civil War era with Harper's Weekly. In the pages of that publication Nast conducted a graphic vendetta against William M. "Boss" Tweed and his corrupt associates in New York City's "Tweed Ring." It has been described by one historian of the subject as "a sustained attack which in its passion and effectiveness stands alone in the history of American graphic art." Another writer explains that the success of the Nast cartoon was achieved "because of the emotional impact of its presentation. It continuously goes beyond the bounds of good taste and conventional manners."

Despite their sometimes caustic nature, from the early cartoon portraying George Washington as an ass down to the present day, graphic depictions and satirical cartoons have played a prominent role in public and political debate. Nast's castigation of the Tweed Ring, Walt McDougall's characterization of presidential candidate James G. Blaine's banquet with the millionaires at Delmonico's as "The Royal Feast of Belshazzar," and numerous other efforts have undoubtedly had an effect on the course and outcome of contemporaneous debate. Lincoln's tall, gangling posture, Teddy Roosevelt's glasses and teeth, and Franklin D. Roosevelt's jutting jaw and cigarette holder have been memorialized by political cartoons with an effect that could not have been obtained by the photographer or the portrait artist. From the viewpoint of history it is clear that our political discourse would have been considerably poorer without them.

[Falwell] contends, however, that the caricature in question here was so "outrageous" as to distinguish it from more traditional political cartoons. There is no doubt that the caricature of [Falwell] and his mother published in Hustler is at best a distant cousin of the political cartoons described above, and a rather poor relation at that. If it were possible by laying down a principled standard to separate the one from the other, public discourse would probably suffer little or no harm. But we doubt that there is any such standard, and we are quite sure that the pejorative description "outrageous" does not supply one. "Outrageousness" in the area of political and social discourse has an inherent subjectiveness about it which would allow a jury to impose liability on the basis of the jurors' tastes or views, or perhaps on the basis of their dislike of a particular expression. An "outrageousness" standard thus runs afoul of our longstanding refusal to allow damages to be awarded because the speech in question may have an adverse emotional impact on the audience. And, as we stated in *FCC v. Pacifica Foundation*:

> "[T]he fact that society may find speech offensive is not a sufficient reason for suppressing it. Indeed, if it is the speaker's opinion that gives offense, that consequence is a reason for according it constitutional protection. For it is a central tenet of the First Amendment that the government must remain neutral in the marketplace of ideas."

Admittedly, these oft-repeated First Amendment principles, like other principles, are subject to limitations. We recognized in *Pacifica Foundation*, that speech that is "'vulgar,' 'offensive,' and 'shocking'" is "not entitled to absolute constitutional protection under all circumstances." In *Chaplinsky v. New Hampshire*, we held that a state could lawfully punish an individual for the use of insulting "'fighting' words - those which by their very utterance inflict injury or tend to incite an immediate breach of the peace." These limitations are but recognition of the observation in *Dun & Bradstreet v. Greenmoss Builders* that this Court has "long recognized that not all speech is of equal First Amendment importance." But the sort of expression involved in this case does not seem to us to be governed by any exception to the general First Amendment principles stated above.

We conclude that public figures and public officials may not recover for the . . . intentional infliction of emotional distress by reason of publications such as the one here at issue without showing in addition that the publication contains a false statement of fact which was made with "actual malice," *i.e.*, with knowledge that the statement was false or with reckless disregard as to whether or not it was true. This is not merely a "blind application" of the *New York Times* standard, it reflects our considered judgment that such a standard is necessary to give adequate "breathing space" to the freedoms protected by the First Amendment.

Here it is clear that [Jerry] Falwell is a "public figure" for purposes of First Amendment law. The jury found against [Falwell] on his libel claim when it decided that the Hustler ad parody could not "reasonably be understood as describing actual facts about [Falwell] or actual events in which [he] participated." The Court of Appeals interpreted the jury's finding to be that the ad parody "was not reasonably believable," and in accordance with our custom we accept this finding. [Falwell] is thus relegated to his claim for damages awarded by the jury for the intentional infliction of emotional distress by "outrageous" conduct. But for [the] reasons heretofore stated this claim cannot, consistently with the First Amendment, form a basis for the award of damages when the conduct in question is the publication of a caricature such as the ad parody involved here. The judgment of the Court of Appeals is accordingly *Reversed.*

The Right To Reply
Miami Herald v. Tornillo

If any newspaper in its columns assails the personal char-
acter or official record of any candidate for election such
newspaper, upon request of such candidate, shall immedi-
ately publish free of cost any reply he may make thereto.
                    - Florida's Right To Reply Law

On September 20, 1972 and again on September 29, 1972
the *Miami Herald* published two editorials highly critical
of Pat Tornillo, a candidate for the Florida House of Representatives.

Tornillo demanded, under Florida's "Right To Reply"
Law, that the *Miami Herald* print, word for word, his editorial reply. Florida's "Right To Reply" Law, enacted in
1903, provided that any candidate for elected office who
is editorially attacked by a newspaper, on either his personal character or official records, be allowed to respond,
free of charge, in print, to the charges made against him.
The *Herald* refused Tornillo's demand to print his reply
to their editorials and Tornillo brought suit against them
in Dade County's Circuit Court to force their compliance.

The *Miami Herald*, in response to Tornillo's suit, asked
the Dade County Court to declare Florida's "Right To Reply" Law an unconstitutional infringement of the First
Amendment's Free Press Clause. The County Court found
for the *Herald*, holding that dictating what a newspaper
must print was no different from dictating what it must
not print. On appeal the Florida Supreme Court overturned this decision, finding for Tornillo and holding the
"Right To Reply" law furthered the free flow of information. The *Herald* appealed to the U.S. Supreme Court.

Oral arguments were heard on April 17, 1974 and the 9-0
decision of the Court was announced on June 25, 1974 by
Chief Justice Warren Burger.

THE MIAMI HERALD COURT

Chief Justice Warren Burger
Appointed Chief Justice by President Nixon
Served 1969 - 1986

Associate Justice William O. Douglas
Appointed by President Franklin Roosevelt
Served 1939 - 1975

Associate Justice William Brennan
Appointed by President Eisenhower
Served 1956 -1990

Associate Justice Potter Stewart
Appointed by President Eisenhower
Served 1958 - 1981

Associate Justice Byron White
Appointed by President Kennedy
Served 1962 - 1993

Associate Justice Thurgood Marshall
Appointed by President Lyndon Johnson
Served 1967 - 1991

Associate Justice Harry Blackmun
Appointed by President Nixon
Served 1970 - 1994

Associate Justice Lewis Powell
Appointed by President Nixon
Served 1971 - 1987

Associate Justice William Rehnquist
Appointed by President Nixon
Served 1971 -

The unedited text of *Miami Herald v. Tornillo* can be found on page 241, volume 418 of *United States Reports.*

MIAMI HERALD v. TORNILLO
June 25, 1974

CHIEF JUSTICE BURGER: The issue in this case is whether a state statute granting a political candidate a right to equal space to reply to criticism and attacks on his record by a newspaper violates the guarantees of a free press.

In the fall of 1972, appellee [Tornillo], Executive Director of the Classroom Teachers Association, apparently a teachers' collective-bargaining agent, was a candidate for the Florida House of Representatives. On September 20, 1972, and again on September 29, 1972, appellant [the Miami Herald] printed editorials critical of [Tornillo]'s candidacy. In response to these editorials [he] demanded that [the Herald] print verbatim his replies, defending the role of the Classroom Teachers Association and the organization's accomplishments for the citizens of Dade County. [The paper] declined to print [his] replies, and [he] brought suit in Circuit Court, Dade County. . . . The action was premised on Florida['s] "right of reply" statute[,] which provides that if a candidate for nomination or election is assailed regarding his personal character or official record by any newspaper, the candidate has the right to demand that the newspaper print, free of cost to the candidate, any reply the candidate may make to the newspaper's charges. The reply must appear in as conspicuous a place and in the same kind of type as the charges which prompted the reply, provided it does not take up more space than the charges. Failure to comply with the statute constitutes a first-degree misdemeanor [a lower offense].

[The Miami Herald] sought a declaration that [the "right of reply" statute] was unconstitutional. After an emergency hearing requested by [Tornillo], the Circuit Court denied injunctive relief because, absent special circumstances, no injunction [court order stopping an act] could properly issue against the commission of a crime, and held that [the statute] was unconstitutional as an infringement on the freedom of the press under the First and Fourteenth Amendments to the Constitution. The Circuit Court concluded that dictating what a newspaper must print was no different from dictating what it must not print. . . .

On direct appeal, the Florida Supreme Court reversed, holding that [the statute] did not violate constitutional guarantees. It held that free speech was enhanced and not abridged by the Florida right-of-reply statute, which in that court's view, furthered the "broad societal interest in the free flow of information to the public." . . .

[The Miami Herald] contends the statute is void . . . because it purports to regulate the content of a newspaper in violation of the First Amendment. . . . It is also contended that the statute fails to distinguish between critical comment which is and which is not defamatory.

[Tornillo] and supporting advocates of an enforceable right of access to the press vigorously argue that government has an obligation to ensure that a wide variety of views reach the public. . . . It is urged that at the time the First Amendment to the Constitution was ratified in 1791 as part of our Bill of Rights the press was broadly representative of the people it was serving. While many of the newspapers were intensely partisan and narrow in their views, the press collectively presented a broad range of opinions to readers. Entry into publishing was inexpensive; pamphlets and books provided meaningful alternatives to the organized press for the expression of unpopular ideas and often treated events and expressed views not covered by conventional newspapers. A true marketplace of ideas existed in which there was relatively easy access to the channels of communication.

Access advocates submit that although newspapers of the present are superficially similar to those of 1791 the press of today is in reality very different from that known in the early years of our national existence. In the past half century a communications revolution has seen the introduction of radio and television into our lives, the promise of a global community through the use of communications satellites, and the specter of a "wired" nation by means of an expanding cable television network with two-way capabilities. The printed press, it is said, has not escaped the effects of this revolution. Newspapers have become big business and there are far fewer of them to serve a larger literate population. Chains of newspapers, national newspapers, national wire and news services, and one-newspaper towns, are the dominant features of a press that has become noncompetitive and enormously powerful and influential in its capacity to manipulate popular opinion and change the course of events. Major metropolitan newspapers have collaborated to establish news services national in scope. Such national news organizations provide syndicated "interpretive reporting" as well as syndicated features and commentary, all of which can serve as part of the new school of "advocacy journalism."

The elimination of competing newspapers in most of our large cities, and the concentration of control of media that results from the only newspaper's being owned by the same interests which own a television station and a radio station, are important components of this trend toward concentration of control of outlets to inform the public.

The result of these vast changes has been to place in a few hands the power to inform the American people and shape public opinion. Much of the editorial opinion and commentary that is printed is that of syndicated columnists distributed nationwide and, as a result, we are told, on national and world issues there tends to be a homogeneity of editorial opinion, commentary, and interpretive analysis. The abuses of bias and manipulative reportage are, likewise, said to be the result of the vast accumulations of unreviewable power in the modern media empires. In effect, it is claimed, the public has lost any ability to respond or to contribute in a meaningful way to the debate on issues. The monopoly of the means of communication allows for little or no critical analysis of the media except in professional journals of very limited readership.

> "This concentration of nationwide news organizations - like other large institutions - has grown increasingly remote from and unresponsive to the popular constituencies on which they depend and which depend on them."

[Tornillo] cites the report of the Commission on Freedom of the Press, chaired by Robert M. Hutchins, in which it was stated, as long ago as 1947, that "[t]he right of free public expression has . . . lost its earlier reality."

The obvious solution, which was available to dissidents at an earlier time when entry into publishing was relatively inexpensive, today would be to have additional newspapers. But the same economic factors which have caused the disappearance of vast numbers of metropolitan news-papers, have made entry into the marketplace of ideas served by the print media almost impossible. It is urged that the claim of newspapers to be "surrogates for the public" carries with it a concomitant fiduciary obligation to account for that stewardship. From this premise it is reasoned that the only effective way to insure fairness and accuracy and to provide for some accountability is for government to take affirmative action. The First Amendment interest of the public in being informed is said to be in peril because the "marketplace of ideas" is today a monopoly controlled by the owners of the market.

Proponents of enforced access to the press take comfort from language in several of this Court's decisions which suggests that the First Amendment acts as a sword as well as a shield, that it imposes obligations on the owners of the press in addition to protecting the press from government regulation. . . .

In *New York Times Co. v. Sullivan,* the Court spoke of "a profound national commitment to the principle that debate on public issues should be uninhibited, robust, and wide-open." It is argued that the "uninhibited, robust" debate is not "wide-open" but open only to a monopoly in control of the press. . . .

The Court foresaw the problems relating to government-enforced access as early as its decision in *Associated Press v. United States.* There it carefully contrasted the private "compulsion to print" called for by the Association's by-laws with the provisions of the District Court decree against appellants which "does not compel AP or its members to permit publication of anything which their 'reason' tells them should not be published." In *Branz-*

burg v. Hayes, we emphasized that the cases then before us "involve no intrusions upon speech or assembly, no prior restraint or restriction on what the press may publish, and no express or implied command that the press publish what it prefers to withhold." . . .

Dissenting in *Pittsburgh Press*, Justice Stewart, joined by Justice Douglas, expressed the view that no "government agency - local, state, or federal - can tell a newspaper in advance what it can print and what it cannot."

[B]eginning with *Associated Press* the Court has expressed sensitivity as to whether a restriction or requirement constituted the compulsion exerted by government on a newspaper to print that which it would not otherwise print. The clear implication has been that any such a compulsion to publish that which "'reason' tells them should not be published" is unconstitutional. A responsible press is an undoubtedly desirable goal, but press responsibility is not mandated by the Constitution and like many other virtues it cannot be legislated.

[Tornillo]'s argument that the Florida statute does not amount to a restriction of [the Miami Herald]'s right to speak because "the statute in question here has not prevented the *Miami Herald* from saying anything it wished" begs the core question. Compelling editors or publishers to publish that which "'reason' tells them should not be published" is what is at issue in this case. The Florida statute operates as a command in the same sense as a statute or regulation forbidding [the Herald] to publish specified matter. Governmental restraint on publishing need not fall into familiar or traditional patterns to be subject to constitutional limitations on governmental powers. The Florida statute exacts a penalty on the basis of the content of a newspaper. The first phase of the penalty resulting from the compelled printing of a reply is exacted in terms of the cost in printing and composing time and materials and in taking up space that could be devoted to other material the newspaper may have preferred to print. It is correct, as [Tornillo] contends, that a newspaper is not subject to the finite technological limitations of time that confront a broadcaster but it is not correct to say that, as an economic reality, a newspaper can proceed to infinite expansion of its column space to accommodate the replies that a government agency determines or a statute commands the readers should have available.

Faced with the penalties that would accrue to any newspaper that published news or commentary arguably within the reach of the right-of-access statute, editors might well conclude that the safe course is to avoid controversy. Therefore, under the operation of the Florida statute, political and electoral coverage would be blunted or reduced. Government-enforced right of access inescapably "dampens the vigor and limits the variety of public debate." ...

Even if a newspaper would face no additional costs to comply with a compulsory access law and would not be forced to forgo publication of news or opinion by the inclusion of a reply, the Florida statute fails to clear the barriers of the First Amendment because of its intrusion into the function of editors. A newspaper is more than a passive receptacle or conduit for news, comment, and advertising. The choice of material to go into a newspaper, and the decisions made as to limitations on the size and content of the paper, and treatment of public issues and public officials - whether fair or unfair - constitute the exercise of editorial control and judgment. It has yet to be demonstrated how governmental regulation of this crucial process can be exercised consistent with First Amendment guarantees of a free press as they have evolved to this time. Accordingly, the judgment of the Supreme Court of Florida is reversed.

Protecting Confidential News Sources
Branzburg v. Hayes

No person shall be compelled to disclose before any Grand Jury any source of information procured or obtained by him and published in a newspaper.
- Kentucky's Reporters' Privilege Law

On November 15, 1969 the Louisville, Kentucky *Courier-Journal* published, under the byline of one of their reporters, Paul Branzburg, a story about the manufacture, sale, and use of illegal drugs in Jefferson County, Kentucky. Branzburg was subpoenaed by the Jefferson County Grand Jury. He was sworn in and asked to identify his confidential sources. He refused to testify, claiming the protection of Kentucky's Reporters' Privilege Law and the First Amendment's Free Press Clause.

On January 10, 1971 the *Courier-Journal* published a second Branzburg article on illegal drugs, this one describing the use of drugs in Frankfort, Kentucky. Branzburg was subpoenaed by the Franklin County Grand Jury to be asked to identify his confidential sources. This time he refused to appear, claiming again the protection of Kentucky's Reporters' Privilege Law and the First Amendment's Free Press Clause.

In both the Jefferson and Franklin County cases, the Kentucky Court of Appeals rejected Branzburg's arguments that his sources were protected under Kentucky's Reporters' Privilege Law and the First Amendment's Free Press Clause, holding that the right of the Grand Juries to investigate violations of state drug laws, to which Branzburg had been a witness, took precedence over his reporter's rights. Branzburg appealed to the U.S. Supreme Court.

Oral arguments were heard on February 26, 1972 and the 5-4 decision of the Court was announced on June 29, 1972 by Associate Justice Byron White.

THE BRANZBURG COURT

Chief Justice Warren Burger
Appointed Chief Justice by President Nixon
Served 1969 - 1986

Associate Justice William O. Douglas
Appointed by President Franklin Roosevelt
Served 1939 - 1975

Associate Justice William Brennan
Appointed by President Eisenhower
Served 1956 -1990

Associate Justice Potter Stewart
Appointed by President Eisenhower
Served 1958 - 1981

Associate Justice Byron White
Appointed by President Kennedy
Served 1962 - 1993

Associate Justice Thurgood Marshall
Appointed by President Lyndon Johnson
Served 1967 - 1991

Associate Justice Harry Blackmun
Appointed by President Nixon
Served 1970 - 1994

Associate Justice Lewis Powell
Appointed by President Nixon
Served 1971 - 1987

Associate Justice William Rehnquist
Appointed by President Nixon
Served 1971 -

The unedited text of *Branzburg v. Hayes* can be found on page 665, volume 408 of *United States Reports.*

THE BRANZBURG CASES
June 29, 1972

JUSTICE WHITE: The issue in these cases is whether requiring newsmen to appear and testify before state or federal grand juries abridges the freedom of speech and press guaranteed by the First Amendment. We hold that it does not.

. . . *Branzburg v. Hayes* and *Branzburg v. Meigs* [bring] before us two judgments of the Kentucky Court of Appeals, both involving petitioner Branzburg, a staff reporter for the Courier-Journal, a daily newspaper published in Louisville, Kentucky.

On November 15, 1969, the Courier-Journal carried a story under [Branzburg]'s by-line describing in detail his observations of two young residents of Jefferson County synthesizing hashish from marihuana, an activity which, they asserted, earned them about $5,000 in three weeks. The article included a photograph of a pair of hands working above a laboratory table on which was a substance identified by the caption as hashish. The article stated that [Branzburg] had promised not to reveal the identity of the two hashish makers. [He] was shortly subpoenaed [ordered to appear and testify] by the Jefferson County grand jury; he appeared, but refused to identify the individuals he had seen possessing marijuana or the persons he had seen making hashish from marihuana. A state trial court judge ordered [Branzburg] to answer these questions and rejected his contention that the Kentucky reporters' privilege statute, the First Amendment of the United States Constitution, or . . . the Kentucky Constitution authorized his refusal to answer. [Branzburg] then [appealed to] the Kentucky Court of Appeals. . . , but the Court of Appeals denied the petition. It held that [Branzburg] had abandoned his First Amendment argument in a supplemental memorandum he had filed and tacitly rejected his argument based on the Kentucky Constitution. It also construed [interpreted] Kentucky['s Reporter's Privilege Statute] as affording a newsman the privilege of refusing to divulge the identity of an informant who supplied him with information, but held that the statute did not permit a reporter to refuse to testify about events he had observed personally, including the identities of those persons he had observed.

The second case involving petitioner Branzburg arose out of his later story published on January 10, 1971, which described in detail the use of drugs in Frankfort, Kentucky. The article reported that in order to provide a comprehensive survey of the "drug scene" in Frankfort, [Branzburg] had "spent two weeks interviewing several dozen drug users in the capital city" and had seen some of them smoking marihuana. A number of conversations with and observations of several unnamed drug users were recounted. Subpoenaed to appear before a Franklin County grand jury "to testify in the matter of violation of statutes concerning use and sale of drugs," petitioner Branzburg moved to quash [annul] the summons; the motion was denied, although an order was issued protecting Branzburg from revealing "confidential associations, sources or information" but requiring that he "answer any questions which concern or pertain to any criminal act, the commission of which was actually observed by [him]." Prior to the time he was slated to appear before the grand jury, [Branzburg argued] that if he were forced to go before the grand jury or to answer questions regarding the identity of informants or disclose information given to him in confidence, his effectiveness as a reporter would be greatly damaged. The Court of Appeals once again denied the requested writs [orders], reaffirming [again upholding] its construction of Kentucky['s Reporter's Privilege Statute], and rejecting [Branzburg]'s claim of a First Amendment privilege. . . . It characterized [Branzburg]'s fear that his ability to obtain news would be destroyed as "so tenuous that it does not, in the opinion of this court, present an issue of abridgement of the freedom of the press within the meaning of that term as used in the Constitution of the United States."

[Branzburg asked us] to review both judgments of the Kentucky Court of Appeals, and we [agreed].

. . . . Branzburg . . . [claims it] may be simply put: that to gather news it is often necessary to agree either not to identify the source of information published or to publish only part of the facts revealed, or both; that if the reporter is nevertheless forced to reveal these confidences to a grand jury, the source so identified and other confidential sources of other reporters will be measurably deterred from furnishing publishable information, all to the detriment of the free flow of information protected by the First Amendment. Although [Branzburg does] not claim an absolute privilege against official interrogation in all circumstances, [he] assert[s] that the reporter should not be forced either to appear or to testify before a grand jury or at a trial until and unless sufficient grounds are shown for believing that the reporter possesses information relevant to a crime the grand jury is investigating, that the information the reporter has is unavailable from other sources, and that the need for the information is sufficiently compelling to override the claimed invasion of First Amendment interests occasioned by the disclosure. Principally relied upon are prior cases emphasizing the importance of the First Amendment guarantees to individual development and to our system of representative government, decisions requiring that official action with adverse impact on First Amendment rights be justified by a public interest that is "compelling" or "paramount," and those precedents establishing the principle that justifiable governmental goals may not be achieved by unduly broad means having an unnecessary impact on protected rights of speech, press, or association. The heart of the claim is that the burden on news gathering resulting from compelling reporters to disclose confidential information outweighs any public interest in obtaining the information.

We do not question the significance of free speech, press, or assembly to the country's welfare. Nor is it suggested that news gathering does not qualify for First Amendment protection; without some protection for seeking out the news, freedom of the press could be eviscerated. But these cases involve no intrusions upon speech or assembly, no prior restraint or restriction on what the press may publish, and no express or implied command that the press publish what it prefers to withhold. No exaction or tax for the privilege of publishing, and no penalty, civil or criminal, related to the content of published material is at issue here. The use of confidential sources by the press is not forbidden or restricted; reporters remain free to seek news from any source by means within the law. No attempt is made to require the press to publish its sources of information or indiscriminately to disclose them on request.

The sole issue before us is the obligation of reporters to respond to grand jury subpoenas as other citizens do and to answer questions relevant to an investigation into the commission of crime. Citizens generally are not constitutionally immune from grand jury subpoenas; and neither the First Amendment nor any other constitutional provision protects the average citizen from disclosing to a grand jury information that he has received in confidence. The claim is, however, that reporters are exempt from these obligations because if forced to respond to subpoenas and identify their sources or disclose other confidences, their informants will refuse or be reluctant to furnish newsworthy information in the future. This asserted burden on news gathering is said to make compelled testimony from newsmen constitutionally suspect and to require a privileged position for them.

It is clear that the First Amendment does not invalidate every incidental burdening of the press that may result from the enforcement of civil or criminal statutes of general applicability. Under prior cases, otherwise valid laws serving substantial public interests may be enforced against the press as against others, despite the possible burden that may be imposed. The Court has emphasized that "[t]he publisher of a newspaper has no special immunity from the application of general laws. He has no special privilege to invade the rights and liberties of others."
. . .

The prevailing view is that the press is not free to publish with impunity everything and anything it desires to publish. Although it may deter or regulate what is said or published, the press may not circulate knowing or reckless falsehoods damaging to private reputation without subjecting itself to liability for damages, including punitive damages, or even criminal prosecution. A newspaper or a journalist may also be punished for contempt of court, in appropriate circumstances.

. . . . It is thus not surprising that the great weight of authority is that newsmen are not exempt from the normal duty of appearing before a grand jury and answering questions relevant to a criminal investigation. At common law, courts consistently refused to recognize the existence of any privilege authorizing a newsman to refuse to reveal confidential information to a grand jury. . . . These courts have applied the presumption against the existence of an asserted testimonial privilege, and have concluded that the First Amendment interest asserted by the newsman was outweighed by the general obligation of a citizen to appear before a grand jury or at trial, pursuant to a subpoena, and give what information he possesses. The opinions of the state courts in [the *Branzburg* cases] are typical of the prevailing view. . . .

The prevailing constitutional view of the newsman's privilege is very much rooted in the ancient role of the grand jury that has the dual function of determining if there is probable cause to believe that a crime has been committed and of protecting citizens against unfounded criminal prosecutions. Grand jury proceedings are constitutionally mandated for the institution of federal criminal prosecutions for capital or other serious crimes, and "its constitutional prerogatives are rooted in long centuries of Anglo-American history." The Fifth Amendment provides that "[n]o person shall be held to answer for a capital, or otherwise infamous crime, unless on a presentment [written notice] or indictment [charge] of a Grand Jury." The adoption of the grand jury "in our Constitution as the sole method for preferring charges in serious criminal cases shows the high place it held as an instrument of justice." Although state systems of criminal procedure differ greatly among themselves, the grand jury is similarly guaranteed by many state constitutions and plays an important role in fair and effective law enforcement in the overwhelming majority of the States. Because its task is to inquire into the existence of possible criminal conduct and to return only well-founded indictments, its investigative powers are necessarily broad. "It is a grand inquest, a body with powers of investigation and inquisition, the scope of whose inquiries is not to be limited narrowly by questions of propriety or forecasts of the probable result of the investigation, or by doubts whether any particular individual will be found properly subject to an accusation of crime." Hence, the grand jury's authority to subpoena witnesses is not only historic, but essential to its task. Although the powers of the grand jury are not unlimited and are subject to the supervision of a judge, the longstanding principle that "the public . . . has a right to every man's evidence," except for those persons protected by a constitutional, common-law, or statutory privilege," is particularly applicable to grand jury proceedings.

A number of States have provided newsmen a statutory privilege of varying breadth, but the majority have not done so, and none has been provided by federal statute. Until now the only testimonial privilege for unofficial witnesses that is rooted in the Federal Constitution is the Fifth Amendment privilege against compelled self-incrimination. We are asked to create another by interpreting the First Amendment to grant newsmen a testimonial privilege that other citizens do not enjoy. This we decline to do. Fair and effective law enforcement aimed at providing security for the person and property of the individual is a fundamental function of government, and the grand jury plays an important, constitutionally mandated role in this process. On the records now before us, we perceive no basis for holding that the public interest in law enforcement and in ensuring effective grand jury proceedings is insufficient to override the consequential, but uncertain, burden on news gathering that is said to result from insisting that reporters, like other citizens, respond to relevant questions put to them in the course of a valid grand jury investigation or criminal trial.

This conclusion itself involves no restraint on what newspapers may publish or on the type or quality of information reporters may seek to acquire, nor does it threaten the vast bulk of confidential relationships between reporters and their sources. Grand juries address themselves to the issues of whether crimes have been committed and who committed them. Only where news sources themselves are implicated in crime or possess information relevant to the grand jury's task need they or the reporter be concerned about grand jury subpoenas. Nothing before us indicates that a large number or percentage of *all* confidential news sources falls into either category and would in any way be deterred by our holding that the Constitution does not, as it never has, exempt the newsman from performing the citizen's normal duty of appearing and furnishing information relevant to the grand jury's task.

The preference for anonymity of those confidential informants involved in actual criminal conduct is presumably a product of their desire to escape criminal prosecution, and this preference, while understandable, is hardly deserving of constitutional protection. It would be frivolous to assert - and no one does in these cases - that the First Amendment, in the interest of securing news or otherwise, confers a license on either the reporter or his news sources to violate valid criminal laws. Although stealing documents or private wiretapping could provide newsworthy information, neither reporter nor source is immune from conviction for such conduct, whatever the impact on the flow of news. Neither is immune, on First Amendment grounds, from testifying against the other, before the grand jury or at a criminal trial. The Amendment does not reach so far as to override the interest of the public in ensuring that neither reporter nor source is invading the rights of other citizens through reprehensible conduct forbidden to all other persons. To assert the contrary proposition

> "is to answer it, since it involves in its very statement the contention that the freedom of the press is the freedom to do wrong with impunity and implies the right to frustrate and defeat the discharge of those governmental duties upon the performance of which the freedom of all, including that of the press, depends. . . . It suffices to say that, however complete is the right of the press to state public things and discuss them, that right, as every other right enjoyed in human society, is subject to the restraints which separate right from wrong-doing."

Thus, we cannot seriously entertain the notion that the First Amendment protects a newsman's agreement to conceal the criminal conduct of his source, or evidence thereof, on the theory that it is better to write about crime than to do something about it. Insofar as any reporter in these cases undertook not to reveal or testify about the crime he witnessed, his claim of privilege under the First Amendment presents no substantial question. The crimes of news sources are no less reprehensible and threatening to the public interest when witnessed by a reporter than when they are not.

There remain those situations where a source is not engaged in criminal conduct but has information suggesting illegal conduct by others. Newsmen frequently receive information from such sources pursuant to a tacit or express agreement to withhold the source's name and suppress any information that the source wishes not published. Such informants presumably desire anonymity in order to avoid being entangled as a witness in a criminal trial or grand jury investigation. They may fear that disclosure will threaten their job security or personal safety or that it will simply result in dishonor or embarrassment.

The argument that the flow of news will be diminished by compelling reporters to aid the grand jury in a criminal investigation is not irrational, nor are the records before us silent on the matter. But we remain unclear how often and to what extent informers are actually deterred from furnishing information when newsmen are forced to testify before a grand jury. The available data indicate that some newsmen rely a great deal on confidential sources and that some informants are particularly sensitive to the threat of exposure and may be silenced if it is held by this Court that, ordinarily, newsmen must testify pursuant to subpoenas, but the evidence fails to demonstrate that there would be a significant constriction of the flow of news to the public if this Court reaffirms the prior common-law and constitutional rule regarding the testimonial obligations of newsmen. Estimates of the inhibiting effect of such subpoenas on the willingness of informants to make disclosures to newsmen are widely divergent and to a great extent speculative. It would be difficult to canvass the views of the informants themselves; surveys of reporters on this topic are chiefly opinions of predicted informant behavior and must be viewed in the light of the professional self-interest of the interviewees. Reliance by the press on confidential informants does not mean that all such sources will in fact dry up because of the later possible appearance of the newsman before a grand jury. The reporter may never be called and if he objects to testifying, the prosecution may not insist. Also, the relationship of many informants to the press is a symbiotic one which is unlikely to be greatly inhibited by the threat of subpoena: quite often, such informants are members of a minority political or cultural group that relies heavily on the media to propagate its views, publicize its aims, and magnify its exposure to the public. Moreover, grand juries characteristically conduct secret proceedings, and law enforcement officers are themselves experienced in dealing with informers, and have their own methods for protecting them without interference with the effective administration of justice. There is little before us indicating that informants whose interest in avoiding exposure is that it may threaten job security, personal safety, or peace of mind, would in fact be in a worse position, or would think they would be, if they risked placing their trust in public officials as well as reporters. We doubt if the informer who prefers anonymity but is sincerely interested in furnishing evidence of crime will always or very often be deterred by the prospect of dealing with those public authorities characteristically charged with the duty to protect the public interest as well as his.

Accepting the fact, however, that an undetermined number of informants not themselves implicated in crime will nevertheless, for whatever reason, refuse to talk to newsmen if they fear identification by a reporter in an official investigation, we cannot accept the argument that the public interest in possible future news about crime from undisclosed, unverified sources must take precedence over the public interest in pursuing and prosecuting those crimes reported to the press by informants and in thus deterring the commission of such crimes in the future.

We note first that the privilege claimed is that of the reporter, not the informant, and that if the authorities independently identify the informant, neither his own reluctance to testify nor the objection of the newsman would shield him from grand jury inquiry, whatever the impact on the flow of news or on his future usefulness as a secret source of information. More important, it is obvious that agreements to conceal information relevant to commission of crime have very little to recommend them from the standpoint of public policy. Historically, the common law recognized a duty to raise the "hue and cry" and report felonies to the authorities. Misprision of a felony - that is, the concealment of a felony "which a man knows, but never assented to . . . [so as to become] either principal or accessory," was often said to be a common-law crime. The first Congress passed a statute, which is still in effect, defining a federal crime of misprision:

> "Whoever, having knowledge of the actual commission of a felony cognizable by a court of the United States, conceals and does not as soon as possible make known the same to some judge or other person in civil or military authority under the United States, shall be [guilty of misprision]."

It is apparent from this statute, as well as from our history and that of England, that concealment of crime and agreements to do so are not looked upon with favor. Such conduct deserves no encomium [praise], and we decline now to afford it First Amendment protection by denigrating the duty of a citizen, whether reporter or informer, to respond to grand jury subpoenas and answer relevant questions put to him.

Of course, the press has the right to abide by its agreement not to publish all the information it has, but the right to withhold news is not equivalent to a First Amendment exemption from the ordinary duty of all other citizens to furnish relevant information to a grand jury performing an important public function. Private restraints on the flow of information are not so favored by the First Amendment that they override all other public interests. As Justice Black declared in another context, "[f]reedom of the press from governmental interference under the First Amendment does not sanction repression of that freedom by private interests."

Neither are we now convinced that a virtually impenetrable constitutional shield, beyond legislative or judicial control, should be forged to protect a private system of informers operated by the press to report on criminal conduct, a system that would be unaccountable to the public, would pose a threat to the citizen's justifiable expectations of privacy, and would equally protect well-intentioned informants and those who for pay or otherwise betray their trust to their employer or associates. The public through its elected and appointed law enforcement officers regularly utilizes informers, and in proper circumstances may assert a privilege against disclosing the identity of these informers. But

> "[t]he purpose of the privilege is the furtherance
> and protection of the public interest in effective
> law enforcement. The privilege recognizes the
> obligation of citizens to communicate their
> knowledge of the commission of crimes to law-

enforcement officials and, by preserving their anonymity, encourages them to perform that obligation."

Such informers enjoy no constitutional protection. Their testimony is available to the public when desired by grand juries or at criminal trials; their identity cannot be concealed from the defendant when it is critical to his case. Clearly, this system is not impervious to control by the judiciary and the decision whether to unmask an informer or to continue to profit by his anonymity is in public, not private, hands. We think that it should remain there and that public authorities should retain the options of either insisting on the informer's testimony relevant to the prosecution of crime or of seeking the benefit of further information that his exposure might prevent.

We are admonished that refusal to provide a First Amendment reporter's privilege will undermine the freedom of the press to collect and disseminate news. But this is not the lesson history teaches us. . . . From the beginning of our country the press has operated without constitutional protection for press informants, and the press has flourished. The existing constitutional rules have not been a serious obstacle to either the development or retention of confidential news sources by the press.

It is said that currently press subpoenas have multiplied, that mutual distrust and tension between press and officialdom have increased, that reporting styles have changed, and that there is now more need for confidential sources, particularly where the press seeks news about minority cultural and political groups or dissident organizations suspicious of the law and public officials. These developments, even if true, are treacherous grounds for a far-reaching interpretation of the First Amendment fastening a nationwide rule on courts, grand juries, and prosecuting officials everywhere. The obligation to testify in response to grand jury subpoenas will not threaten these sources not involved with criminal conduct and without information relevant to grand jury investigations, and we cannot hold that the Constitution places the sources in these two categories either above the law or beyond its reach.

The argument for such a constitutional privilege rests heavily on those cases holding that the infringement of protected First Amendment rights must be no broader than necessary to achieve a permissible governmental purpose. We do not deal, however, with a governmental institution that has abused its proper function, as a legislative committee does when it "expose[s] for the sake of exposure." Nothing in the record indicates that these grand juries were "prob[ing] at will and without relation to existing need." Nor did the grand juries attempt to invade protected First Amendment rights by forcing wholesale disclosure of names and organizational affiliations for a purpose that was not germane to the determination of whether crime has been committed, and the characteristic secrecy of grand jury proceedings is a further protection against the undue invasion of such rights. The investigative power of the grand jury is necessarily broad if its public responsibility is to be adequately discharged.

The requirements of those cases, which hold that a State's interest must be "compelling" or "paramount" to justify even an indirect burden on First Amendment rights, are also met here. As we have indicated, the investigation of crime by the grand jury implements a fundamental governmental role of securing the safety of the person and property of the citizen, and it appears to us that calling reporters to give testimony in the manner and for the reasons that other citizens are called "bears a reasonable relationship to the achievement of the governmental purpose asserted as its justification." If the test is that the government "convincingly show a substantial relation between the information sought and a subject of overriding and compelling state interest," it is quite apparent (1) that the State has the necessary interest in extirpating the traffic in illegal drugs, in forestalling assassination attempts on the President, and in preventing the community from being disrupted by violent disorders endangering both persons and property; and (2) that, based on [Branzburg's] stories . . . , the grand jury called th[is reporter] as they would others - because it was likely that they could supply information to help the government determine whether illegal conduct had occurred and, if it had, whether there was sufficient evidence to return an indictment.

Similar considerations dispose of the reporters' claims that preliminary to requiring their grand jury appearance, the State must show that a crime has been committed and that they possess relevant information not available from other sources, for only the grand jury itself can make this determination. The role of the grand jury as an important instrument of effective law enforcement necessarily includes an investigatory function with respect to determining whether a crime has been committed and who committed it. To this end it must call witnesses, in the manner best suited to perform its task. "When the grand jury is performing its investigatory function into a general problem area . . . society's interest is best served by a thorough and extensive investigation." A grand jury investigation "is not fully carried out until every available clue has been run down and all witnesses examined in every proper way to find if a crime has been committed." Such an investigation may be triggered by tips, rumors, evidence proferred by the prosecutor, or the personal knowledge of the grand jurors. It is only after the grand jury has examined the evidence that a determination of whether the proceeding will result in an indictment can be made.

> "It is impossible to conceive that in such cases the examination of witnesses must be stopped until a basis is laid by an indictment formally proferred, when the very object of the examination is to ascertain who shall be indicted."

We see no reason to hold that th[is reporter], any more than other citizens, should be excused from furnishing information that may help the grand jury in arriving at its initial determinations.

The privilege claimed here is conditional, not absolute; given the suggested preliminary showings and compelling need, the reporter would be required to testify. Presumably, such a rule would reduce the instances in which reporters could be required to appear, but predicting in advance when and in what circumstances they could be compelled to do so would be difficult. Such a rule would also have implications for the issuance of compulsory process to reporters at civil and criminal trials and at legislative hearings. If newsmen's confidential sources are as sensitive as they are claimed to be, the prospect of being unmasked whenever a judge determines the situation justifies it is hardly a satisfactory solution to the problem. For them, it would appear that only an absolute privilege would suffice.

We are unwilling to embark the judiciary on a long and difficult journey to such an uncertain destination. The administration of a constitutional newsman's privilege would present practical and conceptual difficulties of a high order. Sooner or later, it would be necessary to define those categories of newsmen who qualified for the privilege, a questionable procedure in light of the traditional doctrine that liberty of the press is the right of the lonely pamphleteer who uses carbon paper or a mimeograph just as much as of the large metropolitan publisher who utilizes the latest photocomposition methods. Freedom of the press is a "fundamental personal right" which "is not confined to newspapers and periodicals. It necessarily embraces pamphlets and leaflets. . . . The press in its historic connotation comprehends every sort of publication which affords a vehicle of information and opinion." The informative function asserted by representatives of the organized press in the present cases is also performed by lecturers, political pollsters, novelists, academic researchers, and dramatists. Almost any author may quite accurately assert that he is contributing to the flow of information to the public, that he relies on confidential sources of information, and that these sources will be silenced if he is forced to make disclosures before a grand jury.

In each instance where a reporter is subpoenaed to testify, the courts would also be embroiled in preliminary factual and legal determinations with respect to whether the proper predicate had been laid for the reporter's appearance: Is there probable cause to believe a crime has been committed? Is it likely that the reporter has useful information gained in confidence? Could the grand jury obtain the information elsewhere? Is the official interest sufficient to outweigh the claimed privilege?

Thus, in the end, by considering whether enforcement of a particular law served a "compelling" governmental interest, the courts would be inextricably involved in distinguishing between the value of enforcing different criminal laws. By requiring testimony from a reporter in investigations involving some crimes but not in others, they would be making a value judgment that a legislature had declined to make, since in each case the criminal law involved would represent a considered legislative judgment, not constitutionally suspect, of what conduct is liable to criminal prosecution. The task of judges, like other officials outside the legislative branch, is not to make the law but to uphold it in accordance with their oaths.

. . . . Finally, as we have earlier indicated, news gathering is not without its First Amendment protections, and grand jury investigations if instituted or conducted other than in good faith, would pose wholly different issues for resolution under the First Amendment. Official harassment of the press undertaken not for purposes of law enforcement but to disrupt a reporter's relationship with his news sources would have no justification. Grand juries are subject to judicial control. . . . We do not expect courts will forget that grand juries must operate within the limits of the First Amendment as well as the Fifth.

. . . . The decisions in . . . *Branzburg v. Hayes* and *Branzburg v. Meigs* must be affirmed. Here, [Branzburg] refused to answer questions that directly related to criminal conduct that he had observed and written about. The Kentucky Court of Appeals noted that marihuana is defined as a narcotic drug by statute, and that unlicensed possession or compounding of it is a felony punishable by both fine and imprisonment. It held that [Branzburg] "saw the commission of the statutory felonies of unlawful possession of marijuana and the unlawful conversion of it into hashish. . . . [He] may be presumed to have observed similar violations of the state narcotics laws during the research he did for the story that forms the basis of the subpoena in *Branzburg v. Meigs.* In both cases, if what [Branzburg] wrote was true, he had direct information to provide the grand jury concerning the commission of serious crimes. . . .

The Fairness Doctrine
Red Lion Broadcasting v. FCC

When during the presentation of views on a controversial issue of public importance, an attack is made upon the honesty, character or integrity of an identified person the licensee shall offer that person an opportunity to respond.
— **The FCC's Fairness Doctrine**

On November 27, 1964, as part of a "Christian Crusade" series, Pennsylvania radio station WGCB broadcast the political views of the Reverend Billy James Hargis who, during the fifteen minute program, attacked writer Fred Cook, author of the book, "Goldwater - Extremist on the Right." Reverend Hargis used his airtime to say, in part:

> Who is Cook? [He] was fired from the New York *Telegram* after he made a false charge against an unnamed public official. . . . After losing that job, Cook went to work for *The Nation*, one of the most scurrilous publications of the left which has championed many communist causes over many years. . . . Now this is the man who wrote the book to smear and destroy Barry Goldwater.

Cook demanded, under the Federal Communications Commission (FCC)'s Fairness Doctrine, that Red Lion Broadcasting, the licensee of WGCB, give him free and equal time to reply. Red Lion refused. The FCC, in response to Cook's complaint that he had been personally attacked on the public airwaves and then denied the right to reply under the Fairness Doctrine, sued Red Lion. The U.S. Court of Appeals found for the FCC. Red Lion, asserting that the Fairness Doctrine was a violation of their First Amendment rights, appealed to the Supreme Court.

Oral arguments were heard on April 2-3, 1969 and the 8-0 decision of the Court was announced on June 9, 1969 by Associate Justice Byron White.

THE RED LION COURT

Chief Justice Earl Warren
Appointed Chief Justice by President Eisenhower
Served 1953 - 1969

Associate Justice Hugo Black
Appointed by President Franklin Roosevelt
Served 1937 - 1971

Associate Justice William O. Douglas
Appointed by President Franklin Roosevelt
Served 1939 - 1975

Associate Justice John Marshall Harlan
Appointed by President Eisenhower
Served 1955 - 1971

Associate Justice William Brennan
Appointed by President Eisenhower
Served 1956 -1990

Associate Justice Potter Stewart
Appointed by President Eisenhower
Served 1958 - 1981

Associate Justice Byron White
Appointed by President Kennedy
Served 1962 - 1993

Associate Justice Abe Fortas
Appointed by President Lyndon Johnson
Served 1965 - 1969

Associate Justice Thurgood Marshall
Appointed by President Lyndon Johnson
Served 1967 - 1991

The unedited text of *Red Lion Broadcasting v. FCC* can be found on page 367, volume 395 of *U.S. Reports.*

RED LION BROADCASTING v. FCC
June 9, 1969

JUSTICE WHITE: The Federal Communications Commission [FCC] has for many years imposed on radio and television broadcasters the requirement that discussion of public issues be presented on broadcast stations, and that each side of those issues must be given fair coverage. This is known as the fairness doctrine, which originated very early in the history of broadcasting and has maintained its present outlines for some time. It is an obligation whose content has been defined in a long series of FCC rulings in particular cases, and which is distinct from the statutory requirement of . . . the Communications Act that equal time be allotted all qualified candidates for public office. Two aspects of the fairness doctrine, relating to personal attacks in the context of controversial public issues and to political editorializing, were codified more precisely in the form of FCC regulations in 1967. The [case] before us now . . . challenge[s] the constitutional and statutory bases of the doctrine and component rules. [It] involves the application of the fairness doctrine to a particular broadcast.

The Red Lion Broadcasting Company is licensed to operate a Pennsylvania radio station, WGCB. On November 27, 1964, WGCB carried a fifteen-minute broadcast by the Reverend Billy James Hargis as part of a "Christian Crusade" series. A book by Fred J. Cook entitled "Goldwater - Extremist on the Right" was discussed by Hargis, who said that Cook had been fired by a newspaper for making false charges against city officials; that Cook had then worked for a Communist-affiliated publication; that he had defended Alger Hiss and attacked J. Edgar Hoover and the Central Intelligence Agency; and that he had now written a "book to smear and destroy Barry Goldwater." When Cook heard of the broadcast he concluded that he had been personally attacked and demanded free reply time, which the station refused. After an exchange of letters among Cook, Red Lion, and the FCC, the FCC declared that the Hargis broadcast constituted a personal attack on Cook; that Red Lion had failed to meet its obligation under the fairness doctrine . . . to send a tape, transcript, or summary of the broadcast to Cook and offer him reply time; and that the station must provide reply time whether or not Cook would pay for it. On review in the Court of Appeals for the District of Columbia Circuit, the FCC's position was upheld as constitutional and otherwise proper.

. . . . Believing that the specific application of the fairness doctrine in [this case is] authorized by Congress and enhance[s] rather than abridge[s] the freedoms of speech and press protected by the First Amendment, we hold [it] valid and constitutional, . . . affirming [upholding] the judgment [of the court] below. . . .

The history of the emergence of the fairness doctrine and of the related legislation shows that the Commission's action in [this] case did not exceed its authority, and that in adopting the new regulations the Commission was implementing congressional policy rather than embarking on a frolic of its own.

Before 1927, the allocation of frequencies was left entirely to the private sector, and the result was chaos. It quickly became apparent that broadcast frequencies constituted a scarce resource whose use could be regulated and rationalized only by the Government. Without government control, the medium would be of little use because of the cacophony of competing voices, none of which could be clearly and predictably heard. Consequently, the Federal Radio Commission [FRC] was established to allocate frequencies among competing applicants in a manner responsive to the public "convenience, interest, or necessity."

Very shortly thereafter the Commission expressed its view that the "public interest requires ample play for the free and fair competition of opposing views, and the commission believes that the principle applies ... to all discussions of issues of importance to the public." This doctrine was applied through denial of license renewals or construction permits, both by the FRC and its successor FCC. After an extended period during which the licensee was obliged not only to cover and to cover fairly the views of others, but also to refrain from expressing his own personal views, the latter limitation on the licensee was abandoned and the doctrine developed into its present form.

There is a twofold duty laid down by the FCC. . . . The broadcaster must give adequate coverage to public issues, and coverage must be fair in that it accurately reflects the opposing views. This must be done at the broadcaster's own expense if sponsorship is unavailable. Moreover, the duty must be met by programming obtained at the licensee's own initiative if available from no other source. The Federal Radio Commission had imposed these two basic duties on broadcasters since the outset, and in particular respects the personal attack rules and regulations at issue here have spelled them out in greater detail.

When a personal attack has been made on a figure involved in a public issue, [the FCC] ... require[s] that the individual attacked himself be offered an opportunity to respond. . . .

The statutory authority of the FCC to promulgate these regulations derives from the mandate to the "Commission from time to time, as public convenience, interest, or necessity requires" to promulgate "such rules and regulations and prescribe such restrictions and conditions . . . as may be necessary to carry out the provisions of this chapter. . . ." The Commission is specifically directed to consider the demands of the public interest in the course of granting licenses, renewing them, and modifying them. Moreover, the FCC has included among the conditions of the Red Lion license itself the requirement that operation of the station be carried out in the public interest. This mandate to the FCC to assure that broadcasters operate in the public interest is a broad one, a power "not niggardly but expansive," whose validity we have long upheld. It is broad enough to encompass these regulations.

. . . . In 1959 the Congress amended the statutory requirement of [the Communications Act] that equal time be accorded each political candidate to except certain appearances on news programs, but added that this constituted no exception *"from the obligation imposed upon them under this Act to operate in the public interest and to afford reasonable opportunity for the discussion of conflicting views on issues of public importance."* This language makes it very plain that Congress, in 1959, announced that the phrase "public interest," which had been in the Act since 1927, imposed a duty on broadcasters to discuss both sides of controversial public issues. In other words, the amendment vindicated the FCC's general view that the fairness doctrine inhered in the public interest standard. . . . [A] natural conclusion [is] that the public interest language of the Act authorized the Commission to require licensees to use their stations for discussion of public issues, and that the FCC is free to implement this requirement by reasonable rules and regulations which fall short of abridgment of the freedom of speech and press, and of the censorship proscribed [forbidden] by . . . the Act.

. . . . In light of the fact that the "public interest" in broadcasting clearly encompasses the presentation of vigorous debate of controversial issues of importance and concern to the public: the fact that the FCC has rested upon that language from its very inception a doctrine that these issues must be discussed, and fairly; . . . we think the fairness doctrine and its component personal attack and political editorializing regulations are a legitimate exercise of congressionally delegated authority. . . . We cannot say that the FCC's declaratory ruling in *Red Lion* [is] beyond the scope of the congressionally conferred power to assure that stations are operated by those whose possession of a license serves "the public interest."

The broadcasters challenge the fairness doctrine and its specific manifestations in the personal attack and political editorial rules on conventional First Amendment grounds, alleging that the rules abridge their freedom of speech and press. Their contention is that the First Amendment protects their desire to use their allotted frequencies continuously to broadcast whatever they choose, and to exclude whomever they choose from ever using that frequency. No man may be prevented from saying or publishing what he thinks, or from refusing in his speech or other utterances to give equal weight to the views of his opponents. This right, they say, applies equally to broadcasters.

. . . . It is the right of the viewers and listeners, not the right of the broadcasters, which is paramount. It is the purpose of the First Amendment to preserve an uninhibited marketplace of ideas in which truth will ultimately prevail, rather than to countenance monopolization of that market, whether it be by the Government itself or a private licensee. "[S]peech concerning public affairs is more than self-expression; it is the essence of self-government." It is the right of the public to receive suitable access to social, political, esthetic, moral, and other ideas and experiences which is crucial here. That right may not constitutionally be abridged either by Congress or by the FCC.

. . . . [U]nder specified circumstances, a licensee must offer to make available a reasonable amount of broadcast time to those who have a view different from that which has already been expressed on his station. The expression of a political endorsement, or of a personal attack while dealing with a controversial public issue, simply triggers this time sharing. . . . [T]he First Amendment confers no right on licensees to prevent others from broadcasting on "their" frequencies and no right to an unconditional monopoly of a scarce resource which the Government has denied others the right to use.

In terms of constitutional principle, . . . the personal attack and political editorial rules are indistinguishable from the equal-time provision. . . . That provision, which has been part of the law since 1927, has been held valid by this Court as an obligation of the licensee relieving him of any power in any way to prevent or censor the broadcast, and thus insulating him from liability for defamation. The constitutionality of the statute under the First Amendment was unquestioned.

Nor can we say that it is inconsistent with the First Amendment goal of producing an informed public capable of conducting its own affairs to require a broadcaster to permit answers to personal attacks occurring in the course of discussing controversial issues, or to require that the political opponents of those endorsed by the station be given a chance to communicate with the public. Otherwise, station owners and a few networks would have unfettered power to make time available only to the highest bidders, to communicate only their own views on public issues, people and candidates, and to permit on the air only those with whom they agreed. There is no sanctuary in the First Amendment for unlimited private censorship operating in a medium not open to all. "Freedom of the press from governmental interference under the First Amendment does not sanction repression of that freedom by private interests."

It is strenuously argued, however, that if political editorials or personal attacks will trigger an obligation in broadcasters to afford the opportunity for expression to speakers who need not pay for time and whose views are unpalatable to the licensees, then broadcasters will be irresistibly forced to self-censorship and their coverage of controversial public issues will be eliminated or at least rendered wholly ineffective. Such a result would indeed be a serious matter, for should licensees actually eliminate their coverage of controversial issues, the purposes of the doctrine would be stifled.

. . . . That this will occur now seems unlikely, however, since if present licensees should suddenly prove timorous, the Commission is not powerless to insist that they give adequate and fair attention to public issues. It does not violate the First Amendment to treat licensees given the privilege of using scarce radio frequencies as proxies for the entire community, obligated to give suitable time and attention to matters of great public concern. To condition the granting or renewal of licenses on a willingness to present representative community views on controversial issues is consistent with the ends and purposes of those constitutional provisions forbidding the abridgment of freedom of speech and freedom of the press. Congress need not stand idly by and permit those with licenses to ignore the problems which beset the people or to exclude from the airways anything but their own views of fundamental questions. . . .

Licenses to broadcast do not confer ownership of designated frequencies, but only the temporary privilege of using them. Unless renewed, they expire within three years. The statute mandates the issuance of licenses if the "public convenience, interest, or necessity will be served thereby." In applying this standard the Commission for forty years has been choosing licensees based in part on their program proposals. . . .

[Red Lion] embellish[es its] First Amendment arguments with the contention that the regulations are so vague that [its] duties are impossible to discern. Of this point it is enough to say that . . . we cannot conclude that the FCC has been left a free hand to vindicate its own idiosyncratic conception of the public interest or of the requirements of free speech. Past adjudications [judgments] by the FCC give added precision to the regulations; there was nothing vague about the FCC's specific ruling in *Red Lion* that Fred Cook should be provided an opportunity to reply. . . . Moreover, the FCC itself has recognized that the applicability of its regulations to situations beyond the scope of past cases may be questionable, and will not impose sanctions in such cases without warning. We need to approve every aspect of the fairness doctrine to decide [this case], and we will not now pass upon the constitutionality of these regulations by envisioning the most extreme applications conceivable, but will deal with those problems if and when they arise.

. . . . We . . . hold that the Congress and the Commission do not violate the First Amendment when they require a radio or television station to give reply time to answer personal attacks and political editorials.

. . . . In view of the scarcity of broadcast frequencies, the Government's role in allocating those frequencies, and the legitimate claims of those unable without governmental assistance to gain access to those frequencies for expression of their views, we hold the regulations and ruling at issue here are both authorized by statute and constitutional. The judgment of the Court of Appeals in *Red Lion* is affirmed.

Pretrial Publicity
Gannett Co. v. DePasquale

*In all criminal proceedings, the accused shall enjoy the
right to a speedy and public trial, by an impartial jury.*
- The U.S. Constitution's Sixth Amendment

July 16, 1976 was the last day that forty-two-year-old
Wayne Clapp of suburban Rochester, New York, was seen
alive. The facts surrounding Clapp's disappearance and
the subsequent arrest and indictment of two men for his
murder were reported by two local Rochester newspapers,
the *Democrat & Chronicle* and the *Times-Union*, which
sent reporters to cover the pretrial proceedings.

At those proceeding lawyers for the accused argued that
the continuing press coverage by the *Democrat & Chronicle* and the *Times-Union*, both owned by the Gannett
Company, were jeopardizing the rights of the defendants
to a fair trial. They asked Seneca County Judge Daniel
DePasquale to issue an exclusion order barring the press
from the courtroom. Gannett argued that an exclusion order would violate the First Amendment's Free Press
Clause. The Judge, weighing the paper's First Amendment
right to report against the defendant's Sixth Amendment
right to a fair trial, issued the exclusion order. Gannett appealed to the New York State Supreme Court which
found that the Judge had erred. The Judge appealed to the
New York Court of Appeals which found he had acted
within the law. Gannett Company, asserting that the decision of the New York Court of Appeals to uphold Judge
DePasquale's ruling that that the press could be excluded
from pretrial proceedings was a violation of their First
Amendment rights, appealed to the U.S. Supreme Court.

Oral arguments were heard on November 7, 1978 and the
5-4 decision of the Court was announced on July 2, 1979
by Associate Justice Potter Stewart.

THE GANNETT COURT

Chief Justice Warren Burger
Appointed Chief Justice by President Nixon
Served 1969 - 1986

Associate Justice William Brennan
Appointed by President Eisenhower
Served 1956 -1990

Associate Justice Potter Stewart
Appointed by President Eisenhower
Served 1958 - 1981

Associate Justice Byron White
Appointed by President Kennedy
Served 1962 - 1993

Associate Justice Thurgood Marshall
Appointed by President Lyndon Johnson
Served 1967 - 1991

Associate Justice Harry Blackmun
Appointed by President Nixon
Served 1970 - 1994

Associate Justice Lewis Powell
Appointed by President Nixon
Served 1971 - 1987

Associate Justice William Rehnquist
Appointed by President Nixon
Served 1971 -

Associate Justice John Paul Stevens
Appointed by President Ford
Served 1975 -

The unedited text of *Gannett Co. v. DePasquale* can be found on page 368, volume 443 of *United States Reports.*

GANNETT CO. v. DePASQUALE
July 2, 1979

JUSTICE STEWART: The question presented in this case is whether members of the public [represented by the press] have an independent constitutional right to insist upon access to a pretrial judicial proceeding, even though the accused, the prosecutor, and the trial judge all have agreed to the closure of that proceeding in order to assure a fair trial.

Wayne Clapp, aged 42 and residing at Henrietta, a Rochester, N.Y., suburb, disappeared in July 1976. He was last seen on July 16 when, with two male companions, he went out on his boat to fish in Seneca Lake, about 40 miles from Rochester. The two companions returned in the boat the same day and drove away in Clapp's pickup truck. Clapp was not with them. When he failed to return home by July 19, his family reported his absence to the police. An examination of the boat, laced with bullet-holes, seemed to indicate that Clapp had met a violent death aboard it. Police then began an intensive search for the two men. They also began lake-dragging operations in an attempt to locate Clapp's body.

The petitioner, Gannett Co., Inc., publishes two Rochester newspapers, the morning *Democrat & Chronicle* and the evening *Times-Union.* On July 20, each paper carried its first story about Clapp's disappearance. Each reported the few details that were then known and stated that the police were theorizing that Clapp had been shot on his boat and his body dumped overboard. Each stated that the body was missing. The *Times-Union* mentioned the names of respondents Greathouse and Jones and said that Greathouse "was identified as one of the two companions who accompanied Clapp Friday" on the boat; said that the two were aged 16 and 21, respectively; and noted that the police were seeking the two men and Greathouse's wife, also 16.   Accompanying the evening story was a 1959 photograph of Clapp. The report also contained an appeal from the state police for assistance.

Michigan police apprehended Greathouse, Jones, and the woman on July 21. This came about when an interstate bulletin describing Clapp's truck led to their discovery in Jackson County, Michigan, by police who observed the truck parked at a local motel. [Gannett]'s two Rochester papers on July 22 reported the details of the capture. The stories recounted how the Michigan police, after having arrested Jones in a park, used a helicopter and dogs and tracked down Greathouse and the woman in some woods. They recited that Clapp's truck was located near the park.

The stories also stated that Seneca County police theorized that Clapp was shot with his own pistol, robbed, and his body thrown into Seneca Lake.   The articles provided background on Clapp's life, sketched the events surrounding his disappearance, and said that New York had issued warrants for the arrest of the three persons. One of the articles reported that the Seneca County District Attorney would seek to extradite the suspects and would attempt to carry through with a homicide prosecution even if Clapp's body were not found. The paper also quoted the prosecutor as stating, however, that the evidence was still developing and "the case could change." The other story noted that Greathouse and Jones were from Texas and South Carolina, respectively.

Both papers carried stories on July 23.   These revealed that Jones, the adult, had waived extradition and that New

York police had traveled to Michigan and were questioning the suspects. The articles referred to police speculation that extradition of Greathouse and the woman might involve "legalities" because they were only 16 and considered juveniles in Michigan. The morning story provided details of an interview with the landlady from whom the suspects had rented a room while staying in Seneca County at the time Clapp disappeared. It also noted that Greathouse, according to state police, was on probation in San Antonio, Texas, but that the police did not know the details of his criminal record.

The *Democrat & Chronicle* carried another story on the morning of July 24. It stated that Greathouse had led the Michigan police to the spot where he had buried a .357 magnum revolver belonging to Clapp and that the gun was being returned to New York with the three suspects. It also stated that the police had found ammunition at the motel where Greathouse and the woman were believed to have stayed before they were arrested. The story repeated the basic facts known about the disappearance of Clapp and the capture of the three suspects in Michigan. It stated that New York police continued to search Seneca Lake for Clapp's body.

On July 25, the *Democrat & Chronicle* reported that Greathouse and Jones had been arraigned [brought before the court to enter a plea] before a Seneca County Magistrate on second-degree murder charges shortly after their arrival from Michigan; that they and the woman also had been arraigned on charges of second-degree grand larceny; that the three had been committed to the Seneca County jail; that all three had "appeared calm" during the court session; and that the Magistrate had read depositions [sworn statements] signed by three witnesses, one of whom testified to having heard "five or six shots" from the lake on the day of the disappearance, just before seeing Clapp's boat "veer sharply" in the water.

Greathouse, Jones, and the woman were indicted [charged] by a Seneca County grand jury on August 2. The two men were charged, in several counts, with second-degree murder, robbery, and grand larceny. The woman was indicted on one count of grand larceny. Both the *Democrat & Chronicle* and the *Times-Union* on August 3 reported the filing of the indictments. Each story stated that the murder charges specified that the two men had shot Clapp with his own gun, had weighted his body with anchors and tossed it into the lake, and then had made off with Clapp's credit card, gun, and truck. Each reported that the defendants were held without bail, and each again provided background material with details of Clapp's disappearance. The fact that Clapp's body still had not been recovered was mentioned. One report noted that, according to the prosecutor, if the body were not recovered prior to trial, "it will be the first such trial in New York State history." Each paper on that day also carried a brief notice that a memorial service for Clapp would be held that evening in Henrietta. These notices repeated that Greathouse and Jones had been charged with Clapp's murder and that his body had not been recovered.

On August 6, each paper carried a story reporting the details of the arraignments of Greathouse and Jones the day before. The papers stated that both men had pleaded not guilty to all charges. Once again, each story repeated the basic facts of the accusations against the men and noted that the woman was arraigned on a larceny charge. The stories noted that defense attorneys had been given 90 days in which to file pretrial motions.

During this 90-day period, Greathouse and Jones moved to suppress statements made to the police. The ground they asserted was that those statements had been given involuntarily. They also sought to suppress physical evidence seized as fruits of the allegedly involuntary confessions; the primary physical evidence they sought to suppress was the gun to which, as [Gannett]'s newspaper had reported, Greathouse had led the Michigan police.

. . . . [O]n November 4[, Judge DePasquale heard] defense attorneys [argue] that the unabated buildup of adverse publicity had jeopardized the ability of the defendants to receive a fair trial. They thus requested that the public and the press be excluded from the hearing. The District Attorney did not oppose the motion. Although Carol Ritter, a reporter employed by [Gannett], was present in the courtroom, no objection was made at the time. . . . The trial judge granted the motion.

The next day, however, Ritter wrote a letter to the trial judge asserting a "right to cover this hearing," and requesting that "we . . . be given access to the transcript." The judge responded later the same day. He stated that the suppression hearing had concluded and that any decision on immediate release of the transcript had been reserved [set aside]. [Gannett] then moved the court to set aside its exclusionary order.

The trial judge scheduled a hearing on this motion for November 16. . . . At this proceeding, the trial judge stated that, in his view, the press had a constitutional right of access although he deemed it "unfortunate" that no representative of [Gannett] had objected at the time of the closure motion. Despite his acceptance of the existence of this right, however, the judge emphasized that it had to be balanced against the constitutional right of the defendants to a fair trial. After finding on the record that an open suppression hearing would pose a "reasonable probability of prejudice to these defendants," the judge ruled that the interest of the press and the public was outweighed in this case by the defendants' right to a fair trial. The judge thus refused to vacate [throw out] his exclusion order or grant [Gannett] immediate access to a transcript of the pretrial hearing.

The following day, an original proceeding . . . , challenging the closure orders on First, Sixth, and Fourteenth Amendment grounds, was commenced by [Gannett] in the Supreme Court of the State of New York, Appellate Division, Fourth Department. On December 17, 1976, that court held that the exclusionary orders transgressed the public's vital interest in open judicial proceedings and further constituted an unlawful prior restraint in violation of the First and Fourteenth Amendments. It accordingly vacated the trial court's orders.

On appeal, the New York Court of Appeals held that the case was technically moot [no longer pertinent] but, because of the critical importance of the issues involved, [agreed to hear it]. The court noted that under state law, "[c]riminal trials are presumptively open to the public, including the press," but held that this presumption was overcome in this case because of the danger posed to the defendants' ability to receive a fair trial. Thus, the Court of Appeals upheld the exclusion of the press and the public from the pretrial proceeding. Because of the significance of the constitutional questions involved, we granted certiorari [agreed to hear the case].

. . . . This Court has long recognized that adverse publicity can endanger the ability of a defendant to receive a fair trial. To safeguard the due process rights of the accused, a trial judge has an affirmative constitutional duty to minimize the effects of prejudicial pretrial publicity. And because of the Constitution's pervasive concern for these due process rights, a trial judge may surely take protective measures even when they are not strictly and inescapably necessary.

Publicity concerning pretrial suppression hearings such as the one involved in the present case poses special risks of unfairness. The whole purpose of such hearings is to screen out unreliable or illegally obtained evidence and insure that this evidence does not become known to the jury. Publicity concerning the proceedings at a pretrial hearing, however, could influence public opinion against a defendant and inform potential jurors of inculpatory information wholly inadmissible at the actual trial.

The danger of publicity concerning pretrial suppression hearings is particularly acute, because it may be difficult to measure with any degree of certainty the effects of such publicity on the fairness of the trial. After the commencement of the trial itself, inadmissible prejudicial information about a defendant can be kept from a jury by a variety of means. When such information is publicized during a pretrial proceeding, however, it may never be altogether kept from potential jurors. Closure of pretrial proceedings is often one of the most effective methods that a trial judge can employ to attempt to insure that the fairness of a trial will not be jeopardized by the dissemination of such information throughout the community before the trial itself has even begun.

The Sixth Amendment, applicable to the States through the Fourteenth, surrounds a criminal trial with guarantees such as the rights to notice, confrontation, and compulsory process that have as their overriding purpose the protection of the accused from prosecutorial and judicial abuses. Among the guarantees that the Amendment provides to a person charged with the commission of a criminal offense, and to him alone, is the "right to a speedy and public trial, by an impartial jury." The Constitution nowhere mentions any right of access to a criminal trial on the part of the public; its guarantee, like the others enumerated, is personal to the accused.

Our cases have uniformly recognized the public-trial guarantee as one created for the benefit of the defendant. . . .

While the Sixth Amendment guarantees to a defendant in a criminal case the right to a public trial, it does not guarantee the right to compel a private trial. "The ability to waive a constitutional right does not ordinarily carry with it the right to insist upon the opposite of that right." But the issue here is not whether the defendant can compel a private trial. Rather, the issue is whether members of the public have an enforceable right to a public trial that can be asserted independently of the parties in the litigation.

There can be no blinking the fact that there is a strong societal interest in public trials. Openness in court proceedings may improve the quality of testimony, induce unkown witnesses to come forward with relevant testimony, cause all trial participants to perform their duties more conscientiously, and generally give the public an opportunity to observe the judicial system. But there is a strong societal interest in other constitutional guarantees extended to the accused as well. The public, for example, has a definite and concrete interest in seeing that justice is swiftly and fairly administered. Similarly, the public has an interest in having a criminal case heard by a jury, an interest distinct from the defendant's interest in being tried by a jury of his peers.

Recognition of an independent public interest in the enforcement of Sixth Amendment guarantees is a far cry, however, from the creation of a constitutional right on the part of the public. In an adversary system of criminal justice, the public interest in the administration of justice is protected by the participants in the litigation. Thus, because of the great public interest in jury trials as the preferred mode of fact-finding in criminal cases, a defendant cannot waive a jury trial without the consent of the prosecutor and judge. But if the defendant waives his right to a jury trial, and the prosecutor and the judge consent, it could hardly be seriously argued that a member of the public could demand a jury trial because of the societal interest in that mode of fact-finding. Similarly, while a defendant cannot convert his right to a speedy trial into a right to compel an indefinite postponement, a member of the general public surely has no right to prevent a continuance in order to vindicate the public interest in the efficient administration of justice. In short, our adversary system of criminal justice is premised upon the proposition that the public interest is fully protected by the participants in the litigation.

.... For these reasons, we hold that members of the public [represented by the press] have no constitutional right under the Sixth and Fourteenth Amendments to attend criminal trials.

[Gannett] also argues that members of the press and the public have a right of access to the pretrial hearing by reason of the First and Fourteenth Amendments. . . .

[T]he trial court found that the representatives of the press did have a right of access of constitutional dimension, but held, under the circumstances of this case, that this right was outweighed by the defendants' right to a fair trial. In short, the closure decision was based "on an assessment of the competing societal interests involved . . . rather than on any determination that First Amendment freedoms were not implicated."

Furthermore, any denial of access in this case was not absolute but only temporary. Once the danger of prejudice had dissipated, a transcript of the suppression hearing was made available. The press and the public then had a full opportunity to scrutinize the suppression hearing. Unlike the case of an absolute ban on access, therefore, the press here had the opportunity to inform the public of the details of the pretrial hearing accurately and completely. Under these circumstances, any First and Fourteenth Amendment right of [Gannett] to attend a criminal trial was not violated.

We certainly do not disparage the general desirability of open judicial proceedings. But we are not asked here to declare whether open proceedings represent beneficial social policy, or whether there would be a constitutional barrier to a state law that imposed a stricter standard of closure than the one here employed by the New York courts. Rather, we are asked to hold that the Constitution itself gave [Gannett] an affirmative right of access to this pretrial proceeding, even though all the participants in the litigation agreed that it should be closed to protect the fair-trial rights of the defendants.

For all of the reasons discussed in this opinion, we hold that the Constitution provides no such right. Accordingly, the judgment of the New York Court of Appeals is affirmed.

The Juvenile Shield Law
Smith v. Daily Mail

Nor shall the name of any child, in connection with any [juvenile] proceeding, be published in any newspaper without a written order of the court.

- West Virginia's Juvenile Shield Law

On February 9, 1978 in St. Albans, West Virginia, a fourteen-year-old junior high school student shot and killed a fifteen-year-old classmate. Two local newspapers, the Charleston *Daily Mail* and the Charleston *Gazette*, legally obtained the name of the alleged assailant by interviewing eyewitnesses. The *Gazette*, in direct violation of West Virginia's Juvenile Shield Law, which prohibited the publication of the name of a child involved in a crime without prior juvenile court approval, identified the fourteen-year-old by name in their February 10th morning edition. The *Daily Mail*, which on February 9th had withheld publication of the youth's name, followed the lead of the *Gazette* and also published his name.

West Virginia brought criminal charges in the Kanawah County Juvenile Court against the Charleston *Daily Mail* and the Charleston *Gazette* for violating the West Virginia Juvenile Shield Law. The *Daily Mail* and the *Gazette* responded that the law was an unjustified violation of their First Amendment rights. The newspapers argued that they could not be held criminally liable for publishing a legally obtained fact. West Virginia's Supreme Court found that the Juvenile Shield Law violated the First Amendment. Kanawah County Juvenile Court Judge Robert Smith was prohibited by an Order from the West Virginia Supreme Court from enforcing the law. Judge Smith appealed to the United States Supreme Court.

Oral arguments were heard on March 20, 1979 and the 8-0 decision of the Court was announced on June 26, 1979 by Chief Justice Warren Burger.

THE DAILY MAIL COURT

Chief Justice Warren Burger
Appointed Chief Justice by President Nixon
Served 1969 - 1986

Associate Justice William Brennan
Appointed by President Eisenhower
Served 1956 -1990

Associate Justice Potter Stewart
Appointed by President Eisenhower
Served 1958 - 1981

Associate Justice Byron White
Appointed by President Kennedy
Served 1962 - 1993

Associate Justice Thurgood Marshall
Appointed by President Lyndon Johnson
Served 1967 - 1991

Associate Justice Harry Blackmun
Appointed by President Nixon
Served 1970 - 1994

Associate Justice Lewis Powell
Appointed by President Nixon
Served 1971 - 1987

Associate Justice William Rehnquist
Appointed by President Nixon
Served 1971 -

Associate Justice John Paul Stevens
Appointed by President Ford
Served 1975 -

The unedited text of *Smith v. Daily Mail* can be found on page 97, volume 443 of *United States Reports.*

SMITH v. DAILY MAIL
June 26, 1979

CHIEF JUSTICE BURGER: We granted certiorari [agreed to hear the case] to consider whether a West Virginia statute violates the First and Fourteenth Amendments of the United States Constitution by making it a crime for a newspaper to publish, without the written approval of the juvenile court, the name of any youth charged as a juvenile offender.

The challenged West Virginia statute provides:

> "[N]or shall the name of any child, in connection with any proceedings under this chapter, be published in any newspaper without a written order of the court. . . ."

and:

> "A person who violates . . . a provision of this chapter for which punishment has not been specifically provided, shall be guilty of a misdemeanor [a lesser offense], and upon conviction shall be fined not less than ten nor more than one hundred dollars, or confined in jail not less than five days nor more than six months, or both such fine and imprisonment."

On February 9, 1978, a fifteen-year-old student was shot and killed at Hayes Junior High School in St. Albans, West Virginia, a small community located about thirteen miles outside of Charleston, West Virginia. The alleged assailant, a fourteen-year-old classmate, was identified by seven different eyewitnesses and was arrested by police soon after the incident.

The *Charleston Daily Mail* and the *Charleston Gazette*, respondents here, learned of the shooting by monitoring routinely the police band radio frequency; they immediately dispatched reporters and photographers to the junior high school. The reporters for both papers obtained the name of the alleged assailant simply by asking various witnesses, the police, and an assistant prosecuting attorney who were at the school.

The staffs of both newspapers prepared articles for publication about the incident. The *Daily Mail*'s first article appeared in its February 9 afternoon edition. The article did not mention the alleged attacker's name. The editorial decision to omit the name was made because of the statutory prohibition against publication without prior court approval.

The *Gazette* made a contrary editorial decision and published the juvenile's name and picture in an article about the shooting that appeared in the February 10 morning edition of the paper. In addition, the name of the alleged juvenile attacker was broadcast over at least three different radio stations on February 9 and 10. Since the information had become public knowledge, the *Daily Mail* decided to include the juvenile's name in an article in its afternoon paper on February 10.

On March 1, an indictment [charge] against the respondents [the *Daily Mail*] was returned by a grand jury. The indictment alleged that each [paper] knowingly published the name of a youth involved in a juvenile proceeding in violation of West Virginia [law]. [The *Daily Mail*] then . . . petition[ed] the West Virginia Supreme Court of Appeals . . . [and] alleged that the indictment was based on a statute that violated the First and Fourteenth Amendments of the United States Constitution and several provisions of the State's Constitution and requested an order prohibiting the county officials from taking any action on the indictment.

The West Virginia Supreme Court of Appeals . . . held that the statute abridged the freedom of the press. The court reasoned that the statute operated as a prior restraint on speech and that the State's interest in protecting the identity of the juvenile offender did not overcome the heavy presumption against the constitutionality of such prior restraints.

We [agreed to hear the case].

[The newspapers] urge[d] this Court to hold that because [the West Virginia law] requires court approval prior to publication of the juvenile's name it operates as a "prior restraint" on speech. [The newspapers] concede that this statute is not in the classic mold of prior restraint, there being no prior injunction [court order stopping an act] against publication. Nonetheless, they contend that the prior-approval requirement acts in "operation and effect" like a licensing scheme and thus is another form of prior restraint. As such, [they] argue, the statute bears "a 'heavy presumption' against its constitutional validity." They claim that the State's interest in the anonymity of a juvenile offender is not sufficient to overcome that presumption.

[Smith does] not dispute that the statute amounts to a prior restraint on speech. Rather [he takes] the view that even if it is a prior restraint the statute is constitutional because of the significance of the State's interest in protecting the identity of juveniles.

The resolution of this case does not turn on whether the statutory grant of authority to the juvenile judge to permit publication of the juvenile's name is, in and of itself, a prior restraint. First Amendment protection reaches beyond prior restraints . . . and [the papers] acknowledge that the statutory provision for court approval of disclosure actually may have a less oppressive effect on freedom of the press than a total ban on the publication of the child's name.

. . . . Our recent decisions demonstrate that state action to punish the publication of truthful information seldom can satisfy constitutional standards. In *Landmark Communications* we declared unconstitutional a Virginia statute making it a crime to publish information regarding confidential proceedings before a state judicial review commission that heard complaints about alleged disabilities and misconduct of state-court judges. . . .

In *Cox Broadcasting v. Cohn*, we held that damages could not be recovered against a newspaper for publishing the name of a rape victim. The suit had been based on a state statute that made it a crime to publish the name of the victim; the purpose of the statute was to protect the privacy right of the individual and the family. The name of the victim had become known to the public through official court records dealing with the trial of the rapist. In declaring the statute unconstitutional, the Court, speaking through Justice White, reasoned:

"By placing the information in the public domain on official court records, the State must be presumed to have concluded that the public interest was thereby being served. . . . States may not impose sanctions on the publication of truthful information contained in official court records open to public inspection."

One case that involved a classic prior restraint is particularly relevant to our inquiry. In *Oklahoma Publishing Co. v. District Court*, we struck down a state-court injunction prohibiting the news media from publishing the name or photograph of an eleven-year-old boy who was being tried before a juvenile court. The juvenile court judge had permitted reporters and other members of the public to attend a hearing in the case, notwithstanding a state statute closing such trials to the public. The court then attempted to halt publication of the information obtained from that hearing. We held that once the truthful information was "publicly revealed" or "in the public domain" the court could not constitutionally restrain its dissemination.

None of these opinions directly controls [governs] this case; however, all suggest strongly that if a newspaper lawfully obtains truthful information about a matter of public significance then state officials may not constitutionally punish publication of the information, absent a need to further a state interest of the highest order. These cases involved situations where the government itself provided or made possible press access to the information. That factor is not controlling. Here [the newspapers] relied upon routine newspaper reporting techniques to ascertain the identity of the alleged assailant. A free press cannot be made to rely solely upon the sufferance of government to supply it with information. If the information is lawfully obtained, as it was here, the state may not punish its publication except when necessary to further an interest more substantial than is present here.

The sole interest advanced by the State to justify its criminal statute is to protect the anonymity of the juvenile offender. It is asserted that confidentiality will further his rehabilitation because publication of the name may encourage further antisocial conduct and also may cause the juvenile to lose future employment or suffer other consequences for this single offense. In *Davis v. Alaska*, similar arguments were advanced by the State to justify not permitting a criminal defendant to impeach a prosecution witness on the basis of his juvenile record. We said there that "[w]e do not and need not challenge the State's interest as a matter of its own policy in the administration of criminal justice to seek to preserve the anonymity of a juvenile offender." However, we concluded that the State's policy must be subordinated to the defendant's Sixth Amendment right of confrontation. The important rights created by the First Amendment must be considered along with the rights of defendants guaranteed by the Sixth Amendment. Therefore, the reasoning of *Davis* that the constitutional right must prevail over the state's interest in protecting juveniles applies with equal force here.

The magnitude of the State's interest in this statute is not sufficient to justify application of a criminal penalty to [the newspapers]. Moreover, the statute's approach does not satisfy constitutional requirements. The statute does not restrict the electronic media or any form of publication, except "newspapers," from printing the names of youths charged in a juvenile proceeding. In this very case, three radio stations announced the alleged assailant's name before the *Daily Mail* decided to publish it. Thus, even assuming the statute served a state interest of the highest order, it does not accomplish its stated purpose.

In addition, there is no evidence to demonstrate that the imposition of criminal penalties is necessary to protect the confidentiality of juvenile proceedings. As the Brief for [the newspapers] points out . . . , all fifty states have statutes that provide in some way for confidentiality, but only five, including West Virginia, impose criminal penalties on nonparties for publication of the identity of the juvenile. Although every state has asserted a similar interest, all but a handful have found other ways of accomplishing the objective.

. . . . There is no issue before us of unlawful press access to confidential judicial proceedings; there is no issue here of privacy or prejudicial pretrail publicity. At issue is simply the power of a state to punish the truthful publication of an alleged juvenile delinquent's name lawfully obtained by a newspaper. The asserted state interest cannot justify the statute's imposition of criminal sanctions on this type of publication. Accordingly, the judgment of the West Virginia Supreme Court of Appeals is affirmed [upheld].

Gagging The Press
Nebraska Press Association v. Stuart

In all criminal prosecutions, the accused shall enjoy the right to a speedy and public trial, by an impartial jury of the State and district wherein the crime shall have been committed. **- The Constitution's Sixth Amendment**

On October 18, 1975 in the small rural community of Sutherland, Nebraska, six members of the Harry Kellie family were brutally murdered. Arrested the next day for the crime was one Erwin Charles Simants.

The murders and subsequent arrest of a suspect drew intensive media coverage. On October 22nd defense lawyers, joined by the prosecutor's office, both seeking to limit pre-trial publicity that might impair the defendant's Sixth Amendment right to a fair trial by an impartial jury, asked a Lincoln County Court Judge to impose on the press a gag order restricting all pre-trial media coverage. The Judge agreed and issued the requested gag order. In response the Nebraska Press Association, representing the print and broadcast media, appealed to the Nebraska District Court to lift the County Court's gag order. A District Court Judge found "a clear and present danger that pre-trial publicity could impinge upon the defendant's right to a fair trial" and imposed a second, slightly less restrictive gag order. The Press Association, unsatisfied, appealed to the Nebraska Supreme Court which, while modifying slightly the District Court's gag order, let stand its more restrictive elements. The Nebraska Press Association, asserting that any gag order restrictions on media coverage were a violation of their First Amendment Free Press rights, appealed to the United States Supreme Court.

Oral arguments were heard on April 19, 1976 and the 9-0 decision of the Court was announced on June 30, 1976 by Chief Justice Warren Burger.

THE NEBRASKA PRESS COURT

Chief Justice Warren Burger
Appointed Chief Justice by President Nixon
Served 1969 - 1986

Associate Justice William Brennan
Appointed by President Eisenhower
Served 1956 -1990

Associate Justice Potter Stewart
Appointed by President Eisenhower
Served 1958 - 1981

Associate Justice Byron White
Appointed by President Kennedy
Served 1962 - 1993

Associate Justice Thurgood Marshall
Appointed by President Lyndon Johnson
Served 1967 - 1991

Associate Justice Harry Blackmun
Appointed by President Nixon
Served 1970 - 1994

Associate Justice Lewis Powell
Appointed by President Nixon
Served 1971 - 1987

Associate Justice William Rehnquist
Appointed by President Nixon
Served 1971 -

Associate Justice John Paul Stevens
Appointed by President Ford
Served 1975 -

The unedited text of *Nebraska Press Association v. Stuart*
can be found on page 539, volume 427 of *U.S. Reports.*

NEBRASKA PRESS ASSOCIATION
v. STUART
June 30, 1976

CHIEF JUSTICE BURGER: The respondent State District Judge [Stuart] entered an order restraining the petitioners [the Nebraska Press Association] from publishing or broadcasting accounts of confessions or admissions made by the accused or facts "strongly implicative" of the accused in a widely reported murder of six persons. We granted certiorari [agreed to hear the case] to decide whether the entry of such an order . . . violated the constitutional guarantee of freedom of the press.

On the evening of October 18, 1975, local police found the six members of the Henry Kellie family murdered in their home in Sutherland, Nebraska, a town of about eight hundred and fifty people. Police released the description of a suspect, Erwin Charles Simants, to the reporters who had hastened to the scene of the crime. Simants was arrested and arraigned in Lincoln County Court the following morning. . . .

The crime immediately attracted widespread news coverage. . . . Three days after the crime, the County Attorney and Simants' attorney joined in asking the County Court to enter a restrictive order relating to "matters that may or may not be publicly reported or disclosed to the public," because of the "mass coverage by news media" and the "reasonable likelihood of prejudicial news which would make difficult, if not impossible, the impaneling of an impartial jury and tend to prevent a fair trial." . . . The County Court granted the prosecutor's motion for a restrictive order and entered it the next day. . . .

[O]n October 23 [the Nebraska Press Association asked] that the restrictive order imposed by the County Court be vacated [thrown out].... The District Judge ... on October 27 entered his own restrictive order. The judge found "because of the nature of the crimes charged in the complaint that there is a clear and present danger that pretrial publicity could impinge upon the defendant's right to a fair trial." ...

Four days later, on October 31, [the Nebraska Press Association] ... [appealed] to the Nebraska Supreme Court. ... The Nebraska Supreme Court heard oral argument on November 25, and issued its *per curiam* [by the entire court] opinion December 1.

.... Both society and the individual defendant, the court held, had a vital interest in assuring that Simants be tried by an impartial jury. Because of the publicity surrounding the crime, the court determined that this right was in jeopardy.... We [agreed to hear the case] to address the important issues raised by the District Court order as modified by the Nebraska Supreme Court.... We are informed by the parties that since we [agreed to hear the case], Simants has been convicted of murder and sentenced to death. His appeal is pending in the Nebraska Supreme Court.

.... The problems presented by this case are almost as old as the Republic. Neither in the Constitution nor in contemporaneous writings do we find that the conflict between these two important rights was anticipated, yet it is inconceivable that the authors of the Constitution were unaware of the potential conflicts between the right to an unbiased jury and the guarantee of freedom of the press. The unusually able lawyers who helped write the Constitution and later drafted the Bill of Rights were familiar with the historic episode in which John Adams defended British soldiers charged with homicide for firing into a crowd of Boston demonstrators; they were intimately familiar with the clash of the adversary system and the part that passions of the populace sometimes play in influencing potential jurors. They did not address themselves directly to the situation presented by this case; their chief concern was the need for freedom of expression in the political arena and the dialogue in ideas. But they recognized that there were risks to private rights from an unfettered press. Jefferson, for example, writing from Paris in 1786 concerning press attacks on John Jay, stated:

> "In truth it is afflicting that a man who has past his life in serving the public . . . should yet be liable to have his peace of mind so much disturbed by any individual who shall think proper to arraign him in a newspaper. It is however an evil for which there is no remedy. Our liberty depends on the freedom of the press, and that cannot be limited without being lost. . . ."

The speed of communication and the pervasiveness of the modern news media have exacerbated these problems, however, as numerous appeals demonstrate. The trial of Bruno Hauptmann in a small New Jersey community for the abduction and murder of the Charles Lindberghs' infant child probably was the most widely covered trial up to that time, and the nature of the coverage produced widespread public reaction. Criticism was directed at the "carnival" atmosphere that pervaded the community and the courtroom itself. Responsible leaders of press and the legal profession - including other judges - pointed out that much of this sorry performance could have been controlled by a vigilant trial judge and by other public officers subject to the control of the court.

. . . . The Sixth Amendment in terms guarantees "trial, by an impartial jury . . ." in federal criminal prosecutions. Because "trial by jury in criminal cases is fundamental to the American scheme of justice," the Due Process Clause of the Fourteenth Amendment guarantees the same right in state criminal prosecutions.

> "In essence, the right to jury trial guarantees to the criminally accused a fair trial by a panel of impartial, 'indifferent' jurors. . . . 'A fair trial in a fair tribunal is a basic requirement of due process.' In the ultimate analysis, only the jury can strip a man of his liberty or his life. In the language of Lord Coke, a juror must be as 'indifferent as he stands unsworne.' His verdict must be based upon the evidence developed at the trial."

In the overwhelming majority of criminal trials, pretrial publicity presents few unmanageable threats to this important right. But when the case is a "sensational" one tensions develop between the right of the accused to trial by an impartial jury and the rights guaranteed others by the First Amendment. . . .

The state trial judge in the case before us acted responsibly, out of a legitimate concern, in an effort to protect the defendant's right to a fair trail. What we must decide is not simply whether the Nebraska courts erred in seeing the possibility of real danger to the defendant's rights, but whether in the circumstances of this case the means em ployed were foreclosed by another provision of the Constitution.

The First Amendment provides that "Congress shall make no law . . . abridging the freedom . . . of the press," and it is "no longer open to doubt that the liberty of the press, and of speech, is within the liberty safeguarded by the due process clause of the Fourteenth Amendment from invasion by state action." The Court has interpreted these guarantees to afford special protection against orders that prohibit the publication or broadcast of particular information or commentary - orders that impose a "previous" or "prior" restraint on speech. None of our decided cases on prior restraint involved restrictive orders entered to protect a defendant's right to a fair and impartial jury, but the opinions on prior restraint have a common thread relevant to this case.

 . . . . The thread running through all [our past] cases is that prior restraints on speech and publication are the most serious and the least tolerable infringement on First Amendment rights. A criminal penalty or a judgment in a defamation case is subject to the whole panoply of protections afforded by deferring the impact of the judgment until all avenues of appellate review have been exhausted. Only after judgment has become final, correct or otherwise, does the law's sanction become fully operative.

A prior restraint, by contrast and by definition, has an immediate and irreversible sanction. If it can be said that a threat of criminal or civil sanctions after publication "chills" speech, prior restraint "freezes" it at least for the time.

The damage can be particularly great when the prior restraint falls upon the communication of news and commentary on current events. Truthful reports of public judicial proceedings have been afforded special protection against subsequent punishment. For the same reasons the protection against prior restraint should have particular force as applied to reporting of criminal proceedings, whether the crime in question is a single isolated act or a pattern of criminal conduct.

> "A responsible press has always been regarded as the handmaiden of effective judicial administration, especially in the criminal field. Its function in this regard is documented by an impressive record of service over several centuries. The press does not simply publish information about trials but guards against the miscarriage of justice by subjecting the police, prosecutors, and judicial processes to extensive public scrutiny and criticism."

The extraordinary protections afforded by the First Amendment carry with them something in the nature of a fiduciary duty to exercise the protected rights responsibly - a duty widely acknowledged but not always observed by editors and publishers. It is not asking too much to suggest that those who exercise First Amendment rights in newspapers or broadcasting enterprises direct some effort to protect the rights of an accused to a fair trial by unbiased jurors.

. . . . The authors of the Bill of Rights did not undertake to assign priorities as between First Amendment and Sixth Amendment rights, ranking one as superior to the other. In this case, the [Nebraska Press Association] would have us declare the right of an accused subordinate to their right to publish in all circumstances. But if the authors of these guarantees, fully aware of the potential conflicts between them, were unwilling or unable to resolve the issue by assigning to one priority over the other, it is not for us to rewrite the Constitution by undertaking what they declined to do. . . .

The record demonstrates, as the Nebraska courts held, that there was indeed a risk that pretrial news accounts, true or false, would have some adverse impact on the attitudes of those who might be called as jurors. But on the record now before us it is not clear that further publicity, unchecked, would so distort the views of potential jurors that twelve could not be found who would, under proper instructions, fulfill their sworn duty to render a just verdict exclusively on the evidence presented in open court. . . . Reasonable minds can have few doubts about the gravity of the evil pretrial publicity can work, but the probability that it would do so here was not demonstrated with the degree of certainty our cases on prior restraint require.

. . . . Our analysis ends as it began, with a confrontation between prior restraint imposed to protect one vital constitutional guarantee and the explicit command of another that the freedom to speak and publish shall not be abridged. We reaffirm that the guarantees of freedom of expression are not an absolute prohibition under all circumstances, but the barriers to prior restraint remain high and the presumption against its use continues intact. We hold that, with respect to the order entered in this case prohibiting reporting or commentary on judicial proceedings held in public, the barriers have not been overcome; to the extent that this order restrained publication of such material, it is clearly invalid. To the extent that it prohibited publication based on information gained from other sources, we conclude that the heavy burden imposed as a condition to securing a prior restraint was not met and the judgment of the Nebraska Supreme Court is therefore reversed.

Excluding The Press
Richmond Newspapers v. Virginia

In criminal cases the Court may, in its discretion, exclude from the trial any persons whose presence would impair the conduct of a fair trial, provided that the right of the accused to a public trial shall not be violated.
- Virginia's Courtroom Exclusion Statute

John Paul Stevenson had been tried three times for murder in a Hanover County, Virginia Court. The first trial had resulted in a guilty verdict which was overturned on appeal. The second and third trials had resulted in mistrials. These first three trials were open to the public and covered by the press. The fourth trial was set to begin on September 11, 1978. On that date Stevenson's lawyers requested that the Judge issue an exclusion order barring the public and press from the courtroom. The prosecution had no objection and the Judge, exercising his power under the Virginia Courtroom Exclusion Statute, ordered that: "[T]he Courtroom shall be kept clear of all parties except the witnesses when they testify."

Two reporters covering the trial were ordered out. Their employer, the Richmond Newspapers, appealed to the Judge to reconsider his exclusion order, and after a hearing, from which the press was excluded, they were again denied access to the courtroom. The Richmond Newspapers appealed to the Virginia Supreme Court to lift the exclusion order. On July 9, 1979, that Court upheld the Judge and dismissed their appeal. The Richmond Newspapers, asserting that the exclusion order was in violation of their First Amendment Free Press and Free Speech rights, appealed to the United States Supreme Court.

Oral arguments were heard on February 19, 1980 and the 8-1 decision of the Court was announced on July 2, 1980 by Chief Justice Warren Burger.

THE RICHMOND NEWSPAPERS COURT

Chief Justice Warren Burger
Appointed Chief Justice by President Nixon
Served 1969 - 1986

Associate Justice William Brennan
Appointed by President Eisenhower
Served 1956 -1990

Associate Justice Potter Stewart
Appointed by President Eisenhower
Served 1958 - 1981

Associate Justice Byron White
Appointed by President Kennedy
Served 1962 - 1993

Associate Justice Thurgood Marshall
Appointed by President Lyndon Johnson
Served 1967 - 1991

Associate Justice Harry Blackmun
Appointed by President Nixon
Served 1970 - 1994

Associate Justice Lewis Powell
Appointed by President Nixon
Served 1971 - 1987

Associate Justice William Rehnquist
Appointed by President Nixon
Served 1971 -

Associate Justice John Paul Stevens
Appointed by President Ford
Served 1975 -

The unedited text of *Richmond Newspapers v. Virginia* can be found on page 555, volume 448 of *U.S. Reports.*

RICHMOND NEWSPAPERS v. VIRGINIA
July 2, 1980

CHIEF JUSTICE BURGER: The narrow question presented in this case is whether the right of the public and press
to attend criminal trials is guaranteed under the United
States Constitution.

In March 1976, one Stevenson was indicted for [charged
with] the murder of a hotel manager who had been found
stabbed to death on December 2, 1975. Tried promptly in
July 1976, Stevenson was convicted of second-degree murder in the Circuit Court of Hanover County, Virginia.
The Virginia Supreme Court reversed the conviction in
October 1977, holding that a bloodstained shirt purport-
edly belonging to Stevenson had been improperly admitted into evidence.

Stevenson was retried in the same court. This second trial
ended in a mistrial on May 30, 1978, when a juror asked
to be excused after trial had begun and no alternate was
available.

A third trial, which began in the same court on June 6,
1978, also ended in a mistrial. It appears that the mistrial
may have been declared because a prospective juror had
read about Stevenson's previous trials in a newspaper and
had told other prospective jurors about the case before
the retrial began.

Stevenson was tried in the same court for a fourth time
beginning on September 11, 1978. Present in the courtroom when the case was called were appellants Wheeler

and McCarthy, reporters for appellant Richmond News-papers, Inc. Before the trial began, counsel for the defendant moved that it be closed to the public.

. . . . The trial judge, who had presided over two of the three previous trials, asked if the prosecution had any objection to clearing the courtroom. The prosecutor stated he had no objection and would leave it to the discretion of the court. . . . [T]he trial judge then announced: "[T]he statute gives me that power specifically and the defendant has made the motion." He then ordered "that the Courtroom be kept clear of all parties except the witnesses when they testify." The record does not show that any objections to the closure order were made by anyone present at the time, including appellants Wheeler and McCarthy.

Later that same day, however, appellants sought a hearing . . . to vacate [throw out] the closure order. The trial judge granted the request and scheduled a hearing to follow the close of the day's proceedings. When the hearing began, the court ruled that the hearing was to be treated as part of the trial; accordingly, he again ordered the reporters to leave the courtroom, and they complied.

At the closed hearing, counsel for [Richmond Newspapers] . . . pointed out that the court had failed to consider any other, less drastic measures within its power to ensure a fair trial. Counsel for [Richmond Newspapers] argued that constitutional considerations mandated that before ordering closure, the court should first decide that the rights of the defendant could be protected in no other way.

Counsel for defendant Stevenson pointed out that this was the fourth time he was standing trial. He also referred to "difficulty with information between the jurors," and stated that he "didn't want information to leak out," be published by the media, perhaps inaccurately, and then be seen by the jurors. Defense counsel argued that these things, plus the fact that "this is a small community," made this a proper case for closure.

. . . . The prosecutor again declined comment, and the court summed up by saying:

> "I'm inclined to agree with [defense counsel] that, if I feel that the rights of the defendant are infringed in any way, [when] he makes the motion to do something and it doesn't completely override all rights of everyone else, then I'm inclined to go along with the defendant's motion."

The court denied the motion to vacate and ordered the trial to continue the following morning "with the press and public excluded."

What transpired when the closed trial resumed the next day was disclosed in the following manner by an order of the court entered September 12, 1978:

> "[I]n the absence of the jury, [Stevenson] made a Motion that a mis-trial be declared, which motion was taken under advisement.
>
> "At the conclusion of the Commonwealth's evidence, the attorney for [Stevenson] moved the Court to strike the Commonwealth's evidence on

grounds stated to the record, which Motion was sustained [upheld] by the Court.

"And the jury having been excused, the Court doth find the accused NOT GUILTY of Murder, as charged in the Indictment, and he was allowed to depart."

On September 27, 1978, the trial court granted [Richmond Newspaper's] motion to intervene *nunc pro tunc* [retroactively] in the Stevenson case. [Richmond Newspapers] then petitioned the Virginia Supreme Court . . . and filed an appeal from the trial court's closure order. On July 9, 1979, the Virginia Supreme Court . . . denied the petition. . . .

[Richmond Newspapers] then sought review in this Court. . . . [We agreed to hear the case.]

The criminal trial which [Richmond Newspapers] sought to attend has long since ended, and there is some suggestion that the case is moot [no longer relevant]. This Court has frequently recognized, however, that its jurisdiction is not necessarily defeated by the practical termination of a contest which is short-lived by nature. If the underlying dispute is "capable of repetition, yet evading review," it is not moot.

. . . . We begin consideration of this case by noting that the precise issue presented here has not previously been before this Court for decision. In *Gannett v. DePasquale*, the Court was not required to decide whether a right of access to *trials*, as distinguished from hearings on *pre*trial motions, was constitutionally guaranteed. The Court held that the Sixth Amendment's guarantee to the accused of a public trial gave neither the public nor the press an enforceable right of access to a *pre*trial suppression hearing. One concurring opinion specifically emphasized that "a hearing on a motion before trial to suppress evidence is not a *trial* . . . ." Moreover, the Court did not decide whether the First and Fourteenth Amendments guarantee a right of the public to attend trials, nor did the dissenting opinion reach this issue.

In prior cases the Court has treated questions involving conflicts between publicity and a defendant's right to a fair trial; as we observed in *Nebraska Press Association v. Stuart*, "[t]he problems presented by this [conflict] are almost as old as the Republic." But here for the first time the Court is asked to decide whether a criminal trial itself may be closed to the public upon the unopposed request of a defendant, without any demonstration that closure is required to protect the defendant's superior right to a fair trial, or that some other overriding consideration requires closure.

The origins of the proceeding which has become the modern criminal trial in Anglo-American justice can be traced back beyond reliable historical records. We need not here review all details of its development, but a summary of that history is instructive. What is significant for present purposes is that throughout its evolution, the trial has been open to all who cared to observe.

In the days before the Norman Conquest, cases in England were generally brought before moots, such as the local court of the hundred or the county court, which were attended by the freemen of the community. Somewhat like modern jury duty, attendance at these early meetings was compulsory on the part of the freemen, who were called upon to render judgment.

With the gradual evolution of the jury system in the years after the Norman Conquest, the duty of all freemen to attend trials to render judgment was relaxed, but there is no indication that criminal trials did not remain public. When certain groups were excused from compelled attendance, the statutory exemption did not prevent them from attending; Lord Coke observed that those excused "are not compellable to come, but left to their own liberty."

Although there appear to be few contemporary statements on the subject, reports of the Eyre of Kent, a general court held in 1313-1314, evince a recognition of the importance of public attendance apart from the "jury duty" aspect. It was explained that

> "the King's will was that all evil doers should be punished after their deserts, and that justice should be ministered indifferently to rich as to poor; *and for the better accomplishing of this,* he prayed the community of the county *by their attendance* there to lend him their aid in the establishing of a happy and certain peace that should be both for the honour of the realm and for their own welfare."

From these early times, although great changes in courts and procedure took place, one thing remained constant: the public character of the trial at which guilt or innocence was decided. Sir Thomas Smith, writing in 1565 about "the definitive proceedinges in causes criminall," explained that, while the indictment was put in writing as in civil law countries:

> "All the rest is doone openlie in the presence of the Judges, the Justices, the enquest, the prisoner, *and so manie as will or can come so neare as to heare it*, and all depositions [sworn statements] and witnesses given aloude, *that all men may heare from the mouth of the depositors and witnesses what is saide*."

Three centuries later, Sir Frederick Pollock was able to state of the "rule of publicity" that, "[h]ere we have one tradition, at any rate, which has persisted through all changes." "[O]ne of the most conspicuous features of English justice, that all judicial trials are held in open court, to which the public have free access, . . . appears to have been the rule in England from time immemorial."

We have found nothing to suggest that the presumptive openness of the trial, which English courts were later to call "one of the essential qualities of a court of justice," was not also an attribute of the judicial systems of colonial America. In Virginia, for example, such records as there are of early criminal trials indicate that they were open, and nothing to the contrary has been cited. Indeed, when in the mid-1600's the Virginia Assembly felt that the respect due the courts was "by the clamorous unmannerlynes of the people lost, and order, gravity and decoram which should manifest the authority of a court in the court it selfe neglected," the response was not to restrict the openness of the trials to the public, but instead to prescribe rules for the conduct of those attending them.

In some instances, the openness of trials was explicitly recognized as part of the fundamental law of the Colony. The 1677 Concessions and Agreements of West New Jersey, for example, provided:

"That in all publick courts of justice for tryals of causes, civil or criminal, any person or persons, inhabitants of the said Province may freely come into, and attend the said courts, and hear and be present, at all or any such tryals as shall be there had or passed, that justice may not be done in a corner nor in any covert manner."

The Pennsylvania Frame of Government of 1682 also provided "[t]hat all courts shall be open . . . ," and this declaration was reaffirmed in Section 26 of the Constitution adopted by Pennsylvania in 1776.

Other contemporary writings confirm the recognition that part of the very nature of a criminal trial was its openness to those who wished to attend. Perhaps the best indication of this is found in an address to the inhabitants of Quebec which was drafted by a committee consisting of Thomas Cushing, Richard Henry Lee, and John Dickinson and approved by the First Continental Congress on October 26, 1774. This address, written to explain the position of the Colonies and to gain the support of the people of Quebec, is an "exposition of the fundamental rights of the colonists, as they were understood by a representative assembly chosen from all the colonies." Because it was intended for the inhabitants of Quebec, who had been "educated under another form of government" and had only recently become English subjects, it was thought desirable for the Continental Congress to explain "the inestimable advantages of a free English constitution of government, which it is the privilege of all English subjects to enjoy."

> "[One] great right is that of trial by jury. This provides, that neither life, liberty nor property, can be taken from the possessor, until twelve of his unexceptionable countrymen and peers of his vicinage, who from that neighbourhood may reasonably be supposed to be acquainted with his character, and the characters of the witnesses, upon a fair trial, and full enquiry, face to face, *in open Court, before as many of the people as chuse to attend,* shall pass their sentence upon oath against him. . . ."

As we have shown, and as was shown in both the Court's opinion and the dissent in *Gannett,* the historical evidence demonstrates conclusively that at the time when our organic laws were adopted, criminal trials both here and in England had long been presumptively open. This is no quirk of history; rather, it has long been recognized as an indispensable attribute of an Anglo-American trial. . . .

Foreign observers of English criminal procedure in the eighteenth and early nineteenth centuries came away impressed by the very fact that they had been freely admitted to the courts, as many were not in their own homelands. They marveled that "the whole juridical procedure passes in public," and one commentator declared:

> "The main excellence of the English judicature consists in publicity, in the free trial by jury, and in the extraordinary despatch with which business is transacted. The publicity of their proceed-

ings is indeed astonishing. *Free access to the courts is universally granted.*"

. . . . The early history of open trials in part reflects the widespread acknowledgment, long before there were behavioral scientists, that public trials had significant community therapeutic value. Even without such experts to frame the concept in words, people sensed from experience and observation that, especially in the administration of criminal justice, the means used to achieve justice must have the support derived from public acceptance of both the process and its results.

When a shocking crime occurs, a community reaction of outrage and public protest often follows. Thereafter the open processes of justice serve an important prophylactic purpose, providing an outlet for community concern, hostility, and emotion. Without an awareness that society's responses to criminal conduct are underway, natural human reactions of outrage and protest are frustrated and may manifest themselves in some form of vengeful "self-help," as indeed they did regularly in the activities of vigilante "committees" on our frontiers. "The accusation and conviction or acquittal, as much perhaps as the execution of punishment, operat[e] to restore the imbalance which was created by the offense or public charge, to reaffirm the temporarily lost feeling of security and, perhaps, to satisfy that latent 'urge to punish.'"

Civilized societies withdraw both from the victim and the vigilante the enforcement of criminal laws, but they cannot erase from people's consciousness the fundamental, natural yearning to see justice done - or even the urge for retribution. The crucial prophylactic aspects of the administration of justice cannot function in the dark; no community catharsis can occur if justice is "done in a corner [or] in any covert manner." It is not enough to say that results alone will satiate the natural community desire for satisfaction." A result considered untoward may undermine public confidence, and where the trial has been concealed from public view an unexpected outcome can cause a reaction that the system at best has failed and at worst has been corrupted. To work effectively, it is important that society's criminal process "satisfy the appearance of justice," and the appearance of justice can best be provided by allowing people to observe it.

Looking back, we see that when the ancient "town meeting" form of trial became too cumbersome, twelve members of the community were delegated to act as its surrogates, but the community did not surrender its right to observe the conduct of trials. The people retained a "right of visitation" which enabled them to satisfy themselves that justice was in fact being done.

People in an open society do not demand infallibility from their institutions, but it is difficult for them to accept what they are prohibited from observing. When a criminal trial is conducted in the open, there is at least an opportunity both for understanding the system in general and its workings in a particular case:

> "The educative effect of public attendance is a material advantage. Not only is respect for the law increased and intelligent acquaintance acquired with the methods of government, but a strong confidence in judicial remedies is secured which could never be inspired by a system of secrecy."

. . . . Instead of acquiring information about trials by firsthand observation or by word of mouth from those who attended, people now acquire it chiefly through the print and electronic media. In a sense, this validates the media claim of functioning as surrogates for the public. While media representatives enjoy the same right of access as the public, they often are provided special seating and priority of entry so that they may report what people in attendance have seen and heard. This "contribute[s] to public understanding of the rule of law and to comprehension of the functioning of the entire criminal justice system. . . ."

From this unbroken, uncontradicted history, supported by reasons as valid today as in centuries past, we are bound to conclude that a presumption of openness inheres in the very nature of a criminal trial under our system of justice. This conclusion is hardly novel; without a direct holding on the issue, the Court has voiced its recognition of it in a variety of contexts over the years. . . .

[R]ecently in *Gannett v. DePasquale*, both the majority and dissenting opinion agreed that open trials were part of the common-law tradition.

Despite the history of criminal trials being presumptively open since long before the Constitution, the State presses its contention that neither the Constitution nor the Bill of Rights contains any provision which by its terms guarantees to the public the right to attend criminal trials. Standing alone, this is correct, but there remains the question whether, absent an explicit provision, the Constitution affords protection against exclusion of the public from criminal trials.

The First Amendment, in conjunction with the Fourteenth, prohibits governments from "abridging the freedom of speech, or of the press; or the right of the people peaceably to assemble, and to petition the Government for a redress of grievances." These expressly guaranteed freedoms share a common core purpose of assuring freedom of communication on matters relating to the functioning of government. Plainly it would be difficult to single out any aspect of government of higher concern and importance to the people than the manner in which criminal trials are conducted; as we have shown, recognition of this pervades the centuries-old history of open trials and the opinions of this Court.

The Bill of Rights was enacted against the backdrop of the long history of trials being presumptively open. Public access to trials was then regarded as an important aspect of the process itself; the conduct of trials "before as many of the people as chuse to attend" was regarded as one of "the inestimable advantages of a free English constitution of government." In guaranteeing freedoms such as those of speech and press, the First Amendment can be read as protecting the right of everyone to attend trials so as to give meaning to those explicit guarantees. "[T]he First Amendment goes beyond protection of the press and the self-expression of individuals to prohibit government from limiting the stock of information from which members of the public may draw." Free speech carries with it some freedom to listen. "In a variety of contexts this Court has referred to a First Amendment right to 'receive information and ideas.'" What this means in the context of trials is that the First Amendment guarantees of speech and press, standing alone, prohibit government from summarily closing courtroom doors which had long been open to the public at the time that Amendment was adopted.

"For the First Amendment does not speak equivocally. . . . It must be taken as a command of the broadest scope that explicit language, read in the context of a liberty-loving society, will allow."

It is not crucial whether we describe this right to attend criminal trials to hear, see, and communicate observations concerning them as a "right of access," or a "right to gather information," for we have recognized that "without some protection for seeking out the news, freedom of the press could be eviscerated." The explicit, guaranteed rights to speak and to publish concerning what takes place at a trial would lose much meaning if access to observe the trial could, as it was here, be foreclosed arbitrarily.

The right of access to places traditionally open to the public, as criminal trials have long been, may be seen as assured by the amalgam of the First Amendment guarantees of speech and press; and their affinity to the right of assembly is not without relevance. From the outset, the right of assembly was regarded not only as an independent right but also as a catalyst to augment the free exercise of the other First Amendment rights with which it was deliberately linked by the draftsmen. "The right of peaceable assembly is a right cognate to those of free speech and free press and is equally fundamental." People assemble in public places not only to speak or to take action, but also to listen, observe, and learn; indeed, they may "assembl[e] for any lawful purpose." Subject to the traditional time, place, and manner restrictions, streets, sidewalks, and parks are places traditionally open, where First Amendment rights may be exercised; a trial courtroom also is a public place where the people generally - and representatives of the media - have a right to be present, and where their presence historically has been thought to enhance the integrity and quality of what takes place.

The State argues that the Constitution nowhere spells out a guarantee for the right of the public to attend trials, and that accordingly no such right is protected. The possibility that such a contention could be made did not escape the notice of the Constitution's draftsmen; they were concerned that some important rights might be thought disparaged because not specifically guaranteed. It was even argued that because of this danger no Bill of Rights should be adopted. In a letter to Thomas Jefferson in October 1788, James Madison explained why he, although "in favor of a bill of rights," had "not viewed it in an important light" up to that time: "I conceive that in a certain degree . . . the rights in question are reserved by the manner in which the federal powers are granted." He went on to state that "there is great reason to fear that a positive declaration of some of the most essential rights could not be obtained in the requisite latitude."

But arguments such as the State makes have not precluded recognition of important rights not enumerated. Notwithstanding the appropriate caution against reading into the Constitution rights not explicitly defined, the Court has acknowledged that certain unarticulated rights are implicit in enumerated guarantees. For example, the rights of association and of privacy, the right to be presumed innocent, and the right to be judged by a standard of proof beyond a reasonable doubt in a criminal trial, as well as the right to travel, appear nowhere in the Constitution or Bill of Rights. Yet these important but unarticulated rights have nonetheless been found to share constitutional protection in common with explicit guarantees. The concerns expressed by Madison and others have thus been resolved;

fundamental rights, even though not expressly guaranteed, have been recognized by the Court as indispensable to the enjoyment of rights explicitly defined.

We hold that the right to attend criminal trials is implicit in the guarantees of the First Amendment; without the freedom to attend such trials, which people have exercised for centuries, important aspects of freedom of speech and "of the press could be eviscerated."

Having concluded there was a guaranteed right of the public under the First and Fourteenth Amendments to attend the trial of Stevenson's case, we return to the closure order challenged by [Richmond Newspapers]. The Court in *Gannett* made clear that although the Sixth Amendment guarantees the accused a right to a public trial, it does not give a right to a private trial. Despite the fact that this was the fourth trial of the accused, the trial judge made no findings to support closure; no inquiry was made as to whether alternative solutions would have met the need to ensure fairness; there was no recognition of any right under the Constitution for the public or press to attend the trial. In contrast to the pretrial proceeding dealt with in *Gannett*, there exist in the context of the trial itself various tested alternatives to satisfy the constitutional demands of fairness. There was no suggestion that any problems with witnesses could not have been dealt with by their exclusion from the courtroom or their sequestration during the trial. Nor is there anything to indicate that sequestration of the jurors would not have guarded against their being subjected to any improper information. All of the alternatives admittedly present difficulties for trial courts, but none of the factors relied on here was beyond the realm of the manageable. Absent an overriding interest articulated in findings, the trial of a criminal case must be open to the public. Accordingly, the judgment under review is reversed.

Searches and Seizures In Newsrooms
Zurcher v. Stanford Daily

The right of the people to be secure in their persons, houses, papers, and effects, against unreasonable searches and seizures, shall not be violated.

- The U.S. Constitution's Fourth Amendment

On April 9, 1971 in Palo Alto, California, several police officers were injured in a scuffle with protestors at Stanford University. The *Stanford Daily*, the University's student-run newspaper, had reporters and photographers on the scene who witnessed and recorded, but in no way participated in, the violence between police and protestors.

On April 10th the *Stanford Daily* published an article with photographs of the police-protestor clash. The next day Louis Bergra, the Santa Clara County District Attorney, obtained a search warrant for the *Daily*'s newsroom, based on the belief that additional unpublished photographs taken during the fight could be used in the identification and prosecution of the protestors. A Municipal Court Judge issued the search warrant despite the fact that no one in the newsroom was suspected of participating in the assault. On April 12th, the Palo Alto Police, per the orders of Chief James Zurcher, executed the search warrant in the *Daily*'s newsroom.

The *Stanford Daily* sued Palo Alto's Police Chief and District Attorney for violating both their First Amendment Free Speech and Free Press rights and their Fourth Amendment Illegal Search and Seizure rights. The U.S. District Court found for the *Daily*. The U.S. Court of Appeals upheld the lower court's verdict. Zurcher and Bergra appealed to the United States Supreme Court.

Oral arguments were heard on January 17, 1978 and the 6-3 decision of the Court was announced on May 31, 1978 by Associate Justice Byron White.

THE STANFORD DAILY COURT

Chief Justice Warren Burger
Appointed Chief Justice by President Nixon
Served 1969 - 1986

Associate Justice William Brennan
Appointed by President Eisenhower
Served 1956 -1990

Associate Justice Potter Stewart
Appointed by President Eisenhower
Served 1958 - 1981

Associate Justice Byron White
Appointed by President Kennedy
Served 1962 - 1993

Associate Justice Thurgood Marshall
Appointed by President Lyndon Johnson
Served 1967 - 1991

Associate Justice Harry Blackmun
Appointed by President Nixon
Served 1970 - 1994

Associate Justice Lewis Powell
Appointed by President Nixon
Served 1971 - 1987

Associate Justice William Rehnquist
Appointed by President Nixon
Served 1971 -

Associate Justice John Paul Stevens
Appointed by President Ford
Served 1975 -

The unedited text of *Zurcher v. Stanford Daily* can be found on page 547, volume 436 of *U.S. Reports.*

ZURCHER v. STANFORD DAILY
May 31, 1978

JUSTICE WHITE: . . . . Late in the day on Friday, April 9, 1971, officers of the Palo Alto Police Department and of the Santa Clara County Sheriff's Department responded to a call from the director of the Stanford University Hospital requesting the removal of a large group of demonstrators who had seized the hospital's administrative offices and occupied them since the previous afternoon. After several futile efforts to persuade the demonstrators to leave peacefully, more drastic measures were employed. The demonstrators had barricaded the doors at both ends of a hall adjacent to the administrative offices. The police chose to force their way in at the west end of the corridor. As they did so, a group of demonstrators emerged through the doors at the east end and, armed with sticks and clubs, attacked the group of nine police officers stationed there. One officer was knocked to the floor and struck repeatedly on the head; another suffered a broken shoulder. All nine were injured. There were no police photographers at the east doors, and most bystanders and reporters were on the west side. The officers themselves were able to identify only two of their assailants, but one of them did see at least one person photographing the assault at the east doors.

On Sunday, April 11, a special edition of the *Stanford Daily*, a student newspaper published at Stanford University, carried articles and photographs devoted to the hospital protest and the violent clash between demonstrators and police. The photographs carried the byline of a *Daily* staff member and indicated that he had been at the east end of the hospital hallway where he could have photographed the assault on the nine officers. The next day, the Santa Clara County District Attorney's Office secured a warrant [a written order] from the Municipal Court for an immediate search of the *Daily*'s offices for negatives, film, and pictures showing the events and occurrences at the hospital on the evening of April 9. The warrant issued on a finding of "just, probable and reasonable cause for believing that: Negatives and photographs and films, evidence material and relevant to the identity of the perpetrators of felonies, to wit, Battery on a Peace Officer, and Assault with Deadly Weapon, will be located [on the premises of the *Daily*]." The warrant affidavit contained no allegation or indication that members of the *Daily* staff were in any way involved in unlawful acts at the hospital.

The search pursuant to the warrant was conducted later that day by four police officers and took place in the presence of some members of the *Daily* staff. The *Daily*'s photographic laboratories, filing cabinets, desks, and wastepaper baskets were searched. Locked drawers and rooms were not opened. The officers apparently had opportunity to read notes and correspondence during the search; but, contrary to claims of the staff, the officers denied that they had exceeded the limits of the warrant. They had not been advised by the staff that the areas they were searching contained confidential materials. The search revealed only the photographs that had already been published on April 11, and no materials were removed from the *Daily*'s office.

A month later the *Daily* and various members of its staff, respondents here, brought a civil action in the . . . District Court . . . seeking . . . relief . . . against the police officers who conducted the search, the chief of police, the district attorney and one of his deputies, and the judge who had issued the warrant. The complaint alleged that the search of the *Daily*'s office had deprived [them] under color of state law of rights secured to them by the First, Fourth, and Fourteenth Amendments of the United States Constitution.

The District Court denied the request for an injunction but ... granted declaratory relief. ... The District Court ... held that where the innocent object of the search is a newspaper, First Amendment interests are also involved and that such a search is constitutionally permissible "only in the rare circumstance where there is a *clear showing* that (1) important materials will be destroyed or removed from the jurisdiction; *and* (2) a restraining order would be futile." Since these preconditions to a valid warrant had not been satisfied here, the search of the *Daily*'s offices was declared to have been illegal. The Court of Appeals affirmed [upheld]. We [agreed to hear the case]. We reverse.

.... The District Court held, and [the *Daily*] assert[s] here, that whatever may be true of third-party searches generally, where the third party is a newspaper, there are additional factors derived from the First Amendment that justify a nearly *per se* [by itself] rule forbidding the search warrant and permitting only the subpoena *duces tecum* [an order to bring something to the court]. The general submission is that searches of newspaper offices for evidence of crime reasonably believed to be on the premises will seriously threaten the ability of the press to gather, analyze, and disseminate news. This is said to be true for several reasons: First, searches will be physically disruptive to such an extent that timely publication will be impeded. Second, confidential sources of information will dry up, and the press will also lose opportunities to cover various events because of fears of the participants that press files will be readily available to the authorities. Third, reporters will be deterred from recording and preserving their recollections for future use if such information is subject to seizure. Fourth, the processing of news and its dissemination will be chilled by the prospects that searches will disclose internal editorial deliberations. Fifth, the press will resort to self-censorship to conceal its possession of information of potential interest to the police.

It is true that the struggle from which the Fourth Amendment emerged "is largely a history of conflict between the Crown and the press," and that in issuing warrants and determining the reasonableness of a search, state and federal magistrates should be aware that "unrestricted power of search and seizure could also be an instrument for stifling liberty of expression." Where the materials sought to be seized may be protected by the First Amendment, the requirements of the Fourth Amendment must be applied with "scrupulous exactitude." "A seizure reasonable as to one type of material in one setting may be unreasonable in a different setting or with respect to another kind of material." . . .

Neither the Fourth Amendment nor the cases requiring consideration of First Amendment values in issuing search warrants, however, call for imposing the regime ordered by the District Court. Aware of the long struggle between Crown and press and desiring to curb unjustified official intrusions, the Framers took the enormously important step of subjecting searches to the test of reasonableness and to the general rule requiring search warrants issued by neutral magistrates. They nevertheless did not forbid warrants where the press was involved, did not require special showings that subpoenas would be impractical, and did not insist that the owner of the place to be searched, if connected with the press, must be shown to be implicated in the offense being investigated. Further, the prior cases do no more than insist that the courts apply the warrant requirements with particular exactitude when First Amendment interests would be endangered by the search. As we see it, no more than this is required where the warrant requested is for the seizure of criminal evidence reasonably believed to be on the premises occupied by a newspaper. Properly administered, the preconditions for a warrant - probable cause, specificity with respect to the place to be searched and the things to be seized, and overall reasonableness - should afford sufficient protection against the harms that are assertedly threatened by warrants for searching newspaper offices.

There is no reason to believe, for example, that magistrates cannot guard against searches of the type, scope, and intrusiveness that would actually interfere with the timely publication of a newspaper. Nor, if the requirements of specificity and reasonableness are properly applied, policed, and observed, will there be any occasion or opportunity for officers to rummage at large in newspaper files or to intrude into or to deter normal editorial and publication decisions. The warrant issued in this case authorized nothing of this sort. Nor are we convinced, any more than we were in *Branzburg v. Hayes*, that confidential sources will disappear and that the press will suppress news because of fears of warranted searches. Whatever incremental effect there may be in this regard if search warrants, as well as subpoenas, are permissible in proper circumstances, it does not make a constitutional difference in our judgment.

The fact is that [the *Daily* has] pointed to only a very few instances in the entire United States since 1971 involving the issuance of warrants for searching newspaper premises. This reality hardly suggests abuse; and if abuse occurs, there will be time enough to deal with it. Furthermore, the press is not only an important, critical, and valuable asset to society, but it is not easily intimidated - nor should it be.

. . . . [S]urely a warrant to search newspaper premises for criminal evidence such as the one issued here for news photographs taken in a public place carries no realistic threat of prior restraint or of any direct restraint whatsoever on the publication of the *Daily* or on its communication of ideas. The hazards of such warrants can be avoided by a neutral magistrate carrying out his responsibilities under the Fourth Amendment, for he has ample tools at his disposal to confine warrants to search within reasonable limits.

We note finally that if the evidence sought by warrant is sufficiently connected with the crime to satisfy the probable-cause requirement, it will very likely be sufficiently relevant to justify a subpoena. . . . Further, Fifth Amendment and state shield-law objections that might be asserted in opposition to compliance with a subpoena are largely irrelevant to determining the legality of a search warrant under the Fourth Amendment. Of course, the Fourth Amendment does not prevent or advise against legislative or executive efforts to establish nonconstitutional protections against possible abuses of the search warrant procedure, but we decline to reinterpret the

Amendment to impose a general constitutional barrier against warrants to search newspaper premises, to require resort to subpoenas as a general rule, or to demand prior notice and hearing in connection with the issuance of search warrants.

We accordingly reject the reasons given by the District Court and adopted by the Court of Appeals for holding the search for photographs at the *Stanford Daily* to have been unreasonable within the meaning of the Fourth Amendment and in violation of the First Amendment. Nor has anything else presented here persuaded us that the Amendments forbade this search. It follows that the judgment of the Court of Appeals is reversed.

X-Rated Cable Broadcasts
Denver Telecommunications v. FCC

Cable operators shall be permitted to prohibit programming that the cable operator reasonably believes to describe or depict sexual activities in a patently offensive manner as measured by contemporary community standards. - **The 1992 Federal Cable Act**

In 1992, in an effort to protect children from viewing sexually explicit broadcasts over both leased access and public access cable channels, the Congress passed the Cable Television Consumer Protection Act. Three provisions of the Cable Act sought to regulate the broadcasting on those two types of cable channels of sexually-oriented material. The first two provisions allowed cable operators to prohibit programing on either leased or public access channels that the cable operator believed to be sexually offensive as measured by contemporary community standards. The third provision required the cable operator to segregate, onto a single channel, any remaining sexually-oriented programing and block that channel unless a viewer requested access in advance and in writing.

The Federal Communications Commission issued regulations to implement the Cable Act. Several affected groups representing leased and public access channels, including Denver Educational Television and the Alliance for Community Media, challenged the FCC's regulations as a violation of their First Amendment rights. The U.S. Court of Appeals held that all three provisions were consistent with the First Amendment. Denver Educational Television and the Alliance for Community Media appealed to the United States Supreme Court.

Oral arguments were heard on February 21, 1996 and on June 28, 1996 the 6-3 decision of the Court was announced by Associate Justice Stephen Breyer.

THE "X-RATED CABLE" COURT

Chief Justice William Rehnquist
Appointed Chief Justice By President Reagan
Appointed Associate Justice by President Nixon
Served 1971 -

Associate Justice John Paul Stevens
Appointed by President Ford
Served 1975 -

Associate Justice Sandra Day O'Connor
Appointed by President Reagan
Served 1981-

Associate Justice Antonin Scalia
Appointed by President Reagan
Served 1986 -

Associate Justice Anthony Kennedy
Appointed by President Reagan
Served 1988 -

Associate Justice David Souter
Appointed by President Bush
Served 1990 -

Associate Justice Clarence Thomas
Appointed by President Bush
Served 1991 -

Associate Justice Ruth Bader Ginsburg
Appointed by President Clinton
Served 1993 -

Associate Justice Stephen Breyer
Appointed by President Clinton
Served 1994 -

The unedited text of *Denver Telecommunications v. FCC* can be found in volume 518 of *U.S. Reports.*

DENVER TELECOMMUNICATIONS v. FCC
June 28, 1996

JUSTICE BREYER: These cases present First Amendment challenges to three statutory provisions [of the Cable Television Consumer Protection and Competition Act of 1992] that seek to regulate the broadcasting of "patently offensive" sex-related material on cable television. The provisions apply to programs broadcast over cable on what are known as "leased access channels" and "public, educational, or governmental channels." Two of the provisions essentially permit a cable system operator to prohibit the broadcasting of "programming" that the "operator reasonably believes describes or depicts sexual or excretory activities or organs in a patently offensive manner." The remaining provision requires cable system operators to segregate certain "patently offensive" programming, to place it on a single channel, and to block that channel from viewer access unless the viewer requests access in advance and in writing.

We conclude that the first provision - that *permits* the operator to decide whether or not to broadcast such programs on *leased* access channels - is consistent with the First Amendment. The second provision, that *requires* leased channel operators to segregate and to block that programming, and the third provision, applicable to public, educational, and governmental channels, violate the First Amendment, for they are not appropriately tailored to achieve the basic, legitimate objective of protecting children from exposure to "patently offensive" material.

Cable operators typically own a physical cable network used to convey programming over several dozen cable channels into subscribers' houses. Program sources vary from channel to channel. Most channels carry programming produced by independent firms, including "many national and regional cable programming networks that have emerged in recent years," as well as some programming that the system operator itself (or an operator affiliate) may provide. Other channels may simply retransmit through cable the signals of over-the-air broadcast stations. Certain special channels here at issue, called "leased channels" and "public, educational, or governmental channels," carry programs provided by those to whom the law gives special cable system access rights.

A "leased channel" is a channel that federal law requires a cable system operator to reserve for commercial lease by unaffiliated third parties. About ten to fifteen percent of a cable system's channels would typically fall into this category. "[P]ublic, educational, or governmental channels" (which we shall call "public access channels") are channels that, over the years, local governments have required cable system operators to set aside for public, educational, or governmental purposes as part of the consideration an operator gives in return for permission to install cables under city streets and to use public rights-of-way. Between 1984 and 1992 federal law (as had much pre-1984 state law, in respect to public access channels) prohibited cable system operators from exercising *any* editorial control over the content of any program broadcast over either leased or public access channels.

In 1992, in an effort to control sexually explicit programming conveyed over access channels, Congress enacted the three provisions before us. The first two provisions relate to leased channels. The first [Section 10(a)] says:

> "This subsection shall permit a cable operator to enforce prospectively a written and published policy of prohibiting programming that the cable operator reasonably believes describes or depicts sexual or excretory activities or organs in a patently offensive manner as measured by contemporary community standards."

The second provision [Section 10(b)] applicable only to leased channels requires cable operators to segregate and to block similar programming if they decide to permit, rather than to prohibit, its broadcast. The provision tells the Federal Communications Commission (FCC) to promulgate regulations that will

> (a) require "programmers to inform cable operators if the program[ming] would be indecent as defined by Commission regulations";
> (b) require "cable operators to place" such material "on a single channel"; and
> (c) require "cable operators to block such single channel unless the subscriber requests access to such channel in writing."

. . . . The third provision [Section 10(c)] is similar to the first provision, but applies only to public access channels. The relevant statutory section instructs the FCC to promulgate regulations that will "enable a cable operator of a cable system to prohibit the use, on such system, of any channel capacity of any public, educational, or governmental access facility for any programming which contains obscene material, sexually explicit conduct, or material soliciting or promoting unlawful conduct."

. . . . [T]he federal law before us (the statute as implemented through regulations) now *permits* cable operators either to allow or to forbid the transmission of "patently offensive" sex-related materials over both leased and public access channels, and *requires* those operators, at a minimum, to segregate and to block transmission of that same material on leased channels.

Petitioners [Denver Telecommunications], claiming that the three statutory provisions, as implemented by the Commission regulations, violate the First Amendment, sought judicial review . . . in the United States Court of Appeals for the District of Columbia Circuit. A panel of that Circuit agreed with [Denver Telecommunications] that the provisions violated the First Amendment. The entire Court of Appeals, however, heard the case en banc [with all its members] and reached the opposite conclusion. . . . We granted certiorari [agreed to hear the case] to review the en banc Court's First Amendment determinations.

We turn initially to the provision that *permits* cable system operators to prohibit "patently offensive" (or "indecent") programming transmitted over leased access channels. . . .

We recognize that the First Amendment, the terms of which apply to governmental action, ordinarily does not itself throw into constitutional doubt the decisions of private citizens to permit, or to restrict, speech - and this is so *ordinarily* even where those decisions take place within the framework of a regulatory regime such as broadcasting. Were that not so, courts might have to face the difficult, and potentially restrictive, practical task of deciding which, among any number of private parties involved in

providing a program (for example, networks, station owners, program editors, and program producers), is the
"speaker" whose rights may not be abridged, and who is
the speech-restricting "censor."   Furthermore, as this
Court has held, the editorial function itself is an aspect of
"speech," and a court's decision that a private party, say,
the station owner, is a "censor," could itself interfere with
that private "censor's" freedom to speak as an editor.
Thus, not surprisingly, this Court's First Amendment
broadcasting cases have dealt with governmental efforts
to *restrict*, not governmental efforts to provide or to
maintain, a broadcaster's freedom to pick and to choose
programming.

Nonetheless, [Denver Telecommunications], while conced-
ing that this is ordinarily so, point to circumstances that,
in their view, make the analogy with private broadcasters
inapposite and make this case a special one, warranting a
different constitutional result. As a practical matter, they
say, cable system operators have considerably more power
to "censor" program viewing than do broadcasters, for individual communities typically have only one cable system, linking broadcasters and other program providers
with each community's many subscribers. Moreover, concern about system operators' exercise of this considerable
power originally led government - local and federal - to
insist that operators provide leased and public access channels free of operator editorial control. To permit system
operators to supervise programming on leased access channels will create the very private-censorship risk that this
anti-censorship effort sought to avoid. At the same time,
[Denver Telecommunications] add[s], cable systems have
two relevant special characteristics. They are unusually
involved with government, for they depend upon government permission and government facilities (streets,

rights-of-way) to string the cable necessary for their services. And in respect to leased channels, their speech interests are relatively weak because they act less like editors, such as newspapers or television broadcasters, than like common carriers, such as telephone companies.

Under these circumstances, [Denver Telecommunications] conclude[s], Congress' "permissive law," in *actuality*, will abridge their free speech. And this Court should treat that law as a congressionally imposed, content-based, restriction unredeemed as a properly tailored effort to serve a "compelling interest." . . .

The history of this Court's First Amendment jurisprudence [philosophy of law], however, is one of continual development, as the Constitution's general command that "Congress shall make no law . . . abridging the freedom of speech, or of the press," has been applied to new circumstances requiring different adaptations of prior principles and precedents. The essence of that protection is that Congress may not regulate speech except in cases of extraordinary need and with the exercise of a degree of care that we have not elsewhere required. At the same time, our cases have not left Congress or the States powerless to address the most serious problems.

Over the years, this Court has restated and refined these basic First Amendment principles, adopting them more particularly to the balance of competing interests and the special circumstances of each field of application.

This tradition teaches that the First Amendment embodies an overarching commitment to protect speech from Government regulation through close judicial scrutiny, thereby enforcing the Constitution's constraints, but without imposing judicial formulae so rigid that they become a straightjacket that disables Government from responding to serious problems. This Court, in different contexts, has consistently held that the Government may directly regulate speech to address extraordinary problems, where its regulations are appropriately tailored to resolve those problems without imposing an unnecessarily great restriction on speech. . . .

First, the provision before us comes accompanied with an extremely important justification, one that this Court has often found compelling - the need to protect children from exposure to patently offensive sex-related material.

Second, the provision arises in a very particular context - congressional *permission* for cable operators to regulate programming that, but for a previous Act of Congress, would have had no path of access to cable channels free of an operator's control. The First Amendment interests involved are therefore complex, and involve a balance between those interests served by the access requirements themselves (increasing the availability of avenues of expression to programmers who otherwise would not have them), and the disadvantage to the First Amendment interests of cable operators and other programmers (those to whom the cable operator would have assigned the channels devoted to access).

Third, the problem Congress addressed here is remarkably similar to the problem addressed by the FCC in *Pacifica*, and the balance Congress struck is commensurate with the balance we approved there. . . .

All these factors are present here. Cable television broadcasting, including access channel broadcasting, is as "accessible to children" as over-the-air broadcasting, if not more so. Cable television systems, including access channels, "have established a uniquely pervasive presence in the lives of all Americans." "Patently offensive" material from these stations can "confron[t] the citizen" in the "privacy of the home," with little or no prior warning. There is nothing to stop "adults who feel the need" from finding similar programming elsewhere, say, on tape or in theaters. In fact, the power of cable systems to control home program viewing is not absolute. Over-the-air broadcasting and direct broadcast satellites already provide alternative ways for programmers to reach the home, and are likely to do so to a greater extent in the near future.

Fourth, the permissive nature of Section 10(a) means that it likely restricts speech less than, not more than, the ban at issue in *Pacifica*. The provision removes a restriction as to some speakers - namely, cable operators. Moreover, although the provision does create a risk that a program will not appear, that risk is not the same as the certainty that accompanies a governmental ban. In fact, a glance at the programming that cable operators allow on their own (nonaccess) channels suggests that this distinction is not theoretical, but real. Finally, the provision's permissive nature brings with it a flexibility that allows cable operators, for example, not to ban broadcasts, but, say, to rearrange broadcast times, better to fit the desires of adult audiences while lessening the risks of harm to children. In all these respects, the permissive nature of the approach taken by Congress renders this measure appropriate as a means of achieving the underlying purpose of protecting children.

Of course, cable system operators may not always rearrange or reschedule patently offensive programming. Sometimes, as [Denver Telecommunications] fear[s], they may ban the programming instead. But the same may be said of *Pacifica*'s ban. In practice, the FCC's daytime broadcast ban could have become a total ban, depending upon how private operators (programmers, station owners, networks) responded to it. They would have had to decide whether to reschedule the daytime show for nighttime broadcast in light of comparative audience demand and a host of other practical factors that similarly would determine the practical outcomes of the provisions before us. The upshot, in *both* cases, must be uncertainty as to practical consequences - of the governmental ban in the one case and of the permission in the other. . . .

The existence of this complex balance of interests persuades us that the permissive nature of the provision, coupled with its viewpoint-neutral application, is a constitutionally permissible way to protect children from the type of sexual material that concerned Congress, while accommodating both the First Amendment interests served by the access requirements and those served in restoring to cable operators a degree of the editorial control that Congress removed in 1984.

. . . . [A]s this Court pointed out in *Pacifica*, what is "patently offensive" depends on context (the kind of program on which it appears), degree (not "an occasional expletive"), and time of broadcast (a "pig" is offensive in "the parlor" but not the "barnyard"). Programming at two o'clock in the morning is seen by a basically adult audience and the "patently offensive" must be defined with that fact in mind.

. . . . [W]e conclude that Section 10(a) is consistent with the First Amendment.

The statute's second provision significantly differs from the first, for it does not simply permit, but rather requires, cable system operators to restrict speech - by segregating and blocking "patently offensive" sex-related material appearing on leased channels (but not on other channels). In particular, . . . this provision and its implementing regulations require cable system operators to place "patently offensive" leased channel programming on a separate channel; to block that channel; to unblock the channel within thirty days of a subscriber's written request for access; and to reblock the channel within thirty days of a subscriber's request for reblocking. Also, leased channel programmers must notify cable operators of an intended "patently offensive" broadcast up to thirty days before its scheduled broadcast date.

These requirements have obvious restrictive effects. The several up-to-thirty-day delays, along with single channel segregation, mean that a subscriber cannot decide to watch a single program without considerable advance planning and without letting the "patently offensive" channel in its entirety invade his household for days, perhaps weeks, at a time. These restrictions will prevent programmers from broadcasting to viewers who select programs day by day (or, through "surfing," minute by minute); to viewers who would like occasionally to watch a few, but not many, of the programs on the "patently offensive" channel; and to viewers who simply tend to judge a program's value through channel reputation, *i.e.*, by the company it keeps. Moreover, the "written notice" requirement will further restrict viewing by subscribers who fear for their reputations should the operator, advertently or inadvertently, disclose the list of those who wish to watch the "patently offensive" channel. Further, the added costs and burdens that these requirements impose upon a cable system operator may encourage that operator to ban programming that the operator would otherwise permit to run, even if only late at night.

The Government argues that, despite these adverse consequences, the "segregate and block" requirements are lawful because they are "the least restrictive means of realizing" a "compelling interest," namely "protecting the physical and psychological well-being of minors." It adds that, in any event, the First Amendment, as applied in *Pacifica*, "does not require that regulations of indecency on television be subject to the strictest" First Amendment "standard of review."

We agree with the Government that protection of children is a "compelling interest." But we do not agree that the "segregate and block" requirements properly accommodate the speech restrictions they impose and the legitimate objective they seek to attain. . . .

Several circumstances lead us to this conclusion. For one thing, the law, as recently amended, uses other means to protect children from similar "patently offensive" material broadcast on *un*leased cable channels, *i.e.*, broadcast over any of a system's numerous ordinary, or public access, channels. The law, as recently amended, requires cable operators to "scramble or . . . block" such programming on any (unleased) channel "*primarily dedicated* to sexually-oriented programming." In addition, cable operators must honor a subscriber's request to block any, or all, programs on any channel to which he or she does not wish to subscribe. And manufacturers, in the future, will have to make television sets with a so-called "V chip" - a device that will be able automatically to identify and block sexually explicit or violent programs.

.... [T]he new provisions ... do not force the viewer to receive (for days or weeks at a time) all "patently offensive" programming or none; they will not lead the viewer automatically to judge the few by the reputation of the many; and they will not automatically place the occasional viewer's name on a special list. They therefore inevitably lead us to ask why, if they adequately protect children from "patently offensive" material broadcast on ordinary channels, they would not offer adequate protection from similar leased channel broadcasts as well? Alternatively, if these provisions do not adequately protect children from patently offensive material broadcast on ordinary channels, how could one justify more severe leased channel restrictions when (given ordinary channel programming) they would yield so little additional protection for children?

.... We recognize, as the Solicitor General properly points out, that Congress need not deal with every problem at once; and Congress also must have a degree of leeway in tailoring means to ends. But in light of the 1996 statute, it seems fair to say that Congress now has tried to deal with most of the problem. At this point, we can take Congress' different, and significantly less restrictive, treatment of a highly similar problem at least as *some indication* that more restrictive means are not "essential" (or will not prove very helpful).

The record's description [in this case] and discussion of a different alternative, the "lockbox," leads, through a different route, to a similar conclusion. The Cable Communications Policy Act of 1984 required cable operators to provide "upon the request of a subscriber, a device by which the subscriber can prohibit viewing of a particular cable service during periods selected by the subscriber."

This device - the "lockbox" - would help protect children by permitting their parents to "lock out" those programs or channels that they did not want their children to see. The FCC, in upholding the "segregate and block" provisions, said that lockboxes protected children (including, say, children with inattentive parents) less effectively than those provisions. But it is important to understand why that is so.

The Government sets forth the reasons as follows:

> "In the case of lockboxes, parents would have to discover that such devices exist; find out that their cable operators offer them for sale; spend the time and money to buy one; learn how to program the lockbox to block undesired programs; and, finally, exercise sufficient vigilance to ensure that they have, indeed, locked out whatever indecent programming they do not wish their children to view."

We assume the accuracy of this statement. But, the reasons do not show need for a provision as restrictive as the one before us. Rather, they suggest a set of provisions very much like those that Congress [enacted].

No provision, we concede, short of an absolute ban, can offer certain protection against assault by a determined child. We have not, however, generally allowed this fact alone to justify "'reduc[ing] the adult population . . . to . . . only what is fit for children.'" But, leaving that problem aside, the Solicitor General's list of practical difficulties would seem to call, not for "segregate and block" requirements, but, rather, for informational requirements, for a simple coding system, for readily available blocking equipment (perhaps accessible by telephone), for imposing cost burdens upon system operators (who may spread them through subscription fees); or perhaps even for a system that requires lockbox defaults to be set to block certain channels (say, sex-dedicated channels). These kinds of requirements resemble those that Congress has recently imposed upon all but leased channels. For that reason, the "lockbox description" and the discussion of its frailties reinforces our conclusion that the leased channel provision is overly restrictive when measured against the benefits it is likely to achieve. (We add that the record's discussion of the "lockbox" does not explain why the law now treats leased channels more restrictively than ordinary channels.)

There may, of course, be other explanations. Congress may simply not have bothered to change the leased channel provisions when it introduced a new system for other channels. But responses of this sort, like guesses about the comparative seriousness of the problem, are not legally adequate. In other cases, where, as here, the record before Congress or before an agency provides no convincing explanation, this Court has not been willing to stretch the limits of the plausible, to create hypothetical nonobvious explanations in order to justify laws that impose significant restrictions upon speech.

Consequently, we cannot find that the "segregate and block" restrictions on speech are a narrowly, or reasonably, tailored effort to protect children. Rather, they are overly restrictive, "sacrific[ing]" important First Amendment interests for too "speculative a gain." For that reason they are not consistent with the First Amendment.

The statute's third provision, as implemented by FCC regulation, is similar to its first provision, in that it too *permits* a cable operator to prevent transmission of "patently offensive" programming, in this case on public access channels. But there are four important differences.

The first is the historical background. . . . [C]able operators have traditionally agreed to reserve channel capacity for public, governmental, and educational channels as part of the consideration they give municipalities that award them cable franchises. . . . [T]he requirement to reserve capacity for public access channels is similar to the reservation of a public easement, or a dedication of land for streets and parks, as part of a municipality's approval of a subdivision of land. Significantly, these are channels over which cable operators have not historically exercised editorial control. Unlike Section 10(a) therefore, Section 10(c) does not restore to cable operators editorial rights that they once had, and the countervailing First Amendment interest is nonexistent, or at least much diminished.

The second difference is the institutional background that has developed as a result of the historical difference. When a "leased channel" is made available by the operator to a private lessee, the lessee has total control of programming during the leased time slot. Public access channels, on the other hand, are normally subject to complex supervisory systems of various sorts, often with both public and private elements. Municipalities generally provide in their cable franchising agreements for an access channel manager, who is most commonly a nonprofit organization, but may also be the municipality, or, in some instances, the cable system owner. Access channel activity and management are partly financed with public funds - through franchise fees or other payments pursuant to the franchise agreement, or from general municipal funds.

This system of public, private, and mixed nonprofit elements, through its supervising boards and nonprofit or governmental access managers, can set programming policy and approve or disapprove particular programming services. And this system can police that policy by, for example, requiring indemnification by programmers, certification of compliance with local standards, time segregation, adult content advisories, or even by prescreening individual programs. Whether these locally accountable bodies prescreen programming, promulgate rules for the use of public access channels, or are merely available to respond when problems arise, the upshot is the same: there is a locally accountable body capable of addressing the problem, should it arise, of patently offensive programming broadcast to children, making it unlikely that many children will in fact be exposed to programming considered patently offensive in that community.

Third, the existence of a system aimed at encouraging and securing programming that the community considers valuable strongly suggests that a "cable operator's veto" is less likely necessary to achieve the statute's basic objective, protecting children, than a similar veto in the context of leased channels. Of course, the system of access managers and supervising boards can make mistakes, which the operator might in some cases correct with its veto power. Balanced against this potential benefit, however, is the risk that the veto itself may be mistaken; and its use, or threatened use, could prevent the presentation of programming, that, though borderline, is not "patently offensive" to its targeted audience. And this latter threat must bulk large within a system that already has publicly accountable systems for maintaining responsible programs.

Finally, our examination of the legislative history and the record before us is consistent with what common sense suggests, namely that the public/nonprofit programming control systems now in place would normally avoid, minimize, or eliminate any child-related problems concerning "patently offensive" programming. We have found anecdotal references to what seem isolated instances of potentially indecent programming, some of which may well have occurred on leased, not public access channels.

But these few examples do not necessarily indicate a significant nationwide pattern. The Commission itself did not report *any* examples of "indecent programs" on public access channels. Moreover, comments submitted to the FCC undermine any suggestion that prior to 1992 there were significant problems of indecent programming on public access channels.

At most, we have found borderline examples as to which people's judgment may differ, perhaps acceptable in some communities but not others, of the type that [Denver Telecommunications] fear[s] the law might prohibit. It is difficult to see how such borderline examples could show a compelling need, nationally, to protect children from significantly harmful materials. In the absence of a factual basis substantiating the harm and the efficacy of its proposed cure, we cannot assume that the harm exists or that the regulation redresses it.

The upshot, in respect to the public access channels, is a law that could radically change present programming-related relationships among local community and nonprofit supervising boards and access managers, which relationships are established through municipal law, regulation, and contract. In doing so, it would not significantly restore editorial rights of cable operators, but would greatly increase the risk that certain categories of programming (say, borderline offensive programs) will not appear. At the same time, given present supervisory mechanisms, the need for this particular provision, aimed directly at public access channels, is not obvious. Having carefully reviewed the legislative history of the Act, the proceedings before the FCC, the record below, and the submissions of the parties and *amici* [friends of the Court] here, we conclude that the Government cannot sustain its burden of showing that Section 10(c) is necessary to protect children or that it is appropriately tailored to secure that end.

For these reasons, the judgment of the Court of Appeals is affirmed insofar as it upheld Section 10(a); the judgment of the Court of Appeals is reversed insofar as it upheld Sections 10(b) and 10(c). It is so ordered.

THE U.S. CONSTITUTION

PREAMBLE

We the people of the United States, in order to form a more perfect union, establish justice, insure domestic tranquility, provide for the common defense, promote the general welfare, and secure the blessings of liberty to ourselves and our posterity, do ordain and establish this Constitution for the United States of America.

ARTICLE I

Section 1. All legislative powers herein granted shall be vested in a Congress of the United States, which shall consist of a Senate and House of Representatives.

Section 2. (1) The House of Representatives shall be composed of members chosen every second year by the people of several states, and the electors in each state shall have the qualifications requisite for electors of the most numerous branch of the State Legislature.

(2) No person shall be a Representative who shall not have attained to the age of twenty-five years, and been seven years a citizen of the United States, and who shall not, when elected, be an inhabitant of that state in which he shall be chosen.

(3) Representatives and direct taxes shall be apportioned among the several states which may be included within this union, according to their respective numbers, which shall be determined by adding to the whole number of free persons, including those bound to service for a term of years, and excluding Indians not taxed, three-fifths of all other persons. The actual enumeration shall be made

within three years after the first meeting of the Congress of the United States, and within every subsequent term of ten years, in such manner as they shall by law direct. The number of Representatives shall not exceed one for every thirty thousand, but each state shall have at least one Representative; and until such enumeration shall be made, the State of New Hampshire shall be entitled to choose three, Massachusetts eight, Rhode Island and Providence Plantations one, Connecticut five, New York six, New Jersey four, Pennsylvania eight, Delaware one, Maryland six, Virginia ten, North Carolina five, South Carolina five, and Georgia three.

(4) When vacancies happen in the representation from any state, the executive authority thereof shall issue Writs of Election to fill such vacancies.

(5) The House of Representatives shall choose their Speaker and other Officers; and shall have the sole power of impeachment.

Section 3. (1) The Senate of the United States shall be composed of two Senators from each state, chosen by the legislature thereof, for six years; and each Senator shall have one vote.

(2) Immediately after they shall be assembled in consequence of the first election, they shall be divided as equally as may be into three classes. The seats of the Senators of the first class shall be vacated at the expiration of the second year, of the second class at the expiration of the fourth year, and of the third class at the expiration of the sixth year, so that one-third may be chosen every second year; and if vacancies happen by resignation, or otherwise, during the recess of the legislature of any state, the execu-

tive thereof may make temporary appointments until the next meeting of the legislature, which shall then fill such vacancies.

(3) No person shall be a Senator who shall not have attained to the age of thirty years, and been nine years a citizen of the United States, and who shall not, when elected, be an inhabitant of that state for which he shall be chosen.

(4) The Vice President of the United States shall be President of the Senate, but shall have no vote, unless they be equally divided.

(5) The Senate shall choose their other Officers, and also a President pro tempore, in the absence of the Vice President, or when he shall exercise the Office of President of the United States.

(6) The Senate shall have the sole power to try all impeachments. When sitting for that purpose, they shall be on oath or affirmation. When the President of the United States is tried, the Chief Justice shall preside: and no person shall be convicted without the concurrence of two-thirds of the members present.

(7) Judgment in cases of impeachment shall not extend further than to removal from office, and disqualification to hold and enjoy any office of honor, trust, or profit under the United States: but the party convicted shall nevertheless be liable and subject to indictment, trial, judgment, and punishment, according to law.

Section 4. (1) The times, places and manner of holding elections for Senators and Representatives, shall be prescribed in each state by the legislature thereof; but the Congress may at any time by law make or alter such regulations, except as to the places of choosing Senators.

(2) The Congress shall assemble at least once in every year, and such meeting shall be on the first Monday in December, unless they shall by law appoint a different day.

Section 5. (1) Each House shall be the judge of the elections, returns, and qualifications of its own members, and a majority of each shall constitute a quorum to do business; but a smaller number may adjourn from day to day, and may be authorized to compel the attendance of absent members, in such manner, and under such penalties as each House may provide.

(2) Each House may determine the rules of its proceedings, punish its members for disorderly behavior, and, with the concurrence of two-thirds, expel a member.

(3) Each House shall keep a journal of its proceedings, and from time to time publish the same, excepting such parts as may in their judgment require secrecy; and the yeas and nays of the members of either House on any question shall, at the desire of one-fifth of those present, be entered on the journal.

(4) Neither House, during the Session of Congress, shall, without the consent of the other, adjourn for more than three days, nor to any other place than that in which the two Houses shall be sitting.

Section 6. (1) The Senators and Representatives shall receive a compensation for their services, to be ascertained by law, and paid out of the Treasury of the United States. They shall in all cases, except treason, felony and breach of the peace, be privileged from arrest during their attendance at the session of their respective Houses, and in going to and returning from the same; and for any speech or debate in either House, they shall not be questioned in any other place.

(2) No Senator or Representative shall, during the time for which he was elected, be appointed to any civil office under the authority of the United States, which shall have been created, or the emoluments whereof shall have been increased during such time and no person holding any office under the United States, shall be a member of either House during his continuance in office.

Section 7. (1) All bills for raising revenue shall originate in the House of Representatives; but the Senate may propose or concur with amendments as on other bills.

(2) Every bill which shall have passed the House of Representatives and the Senate, shall, before it become a law, be presented to the President of the United States; if he approve he shall sign it, but if not he shall return it, with his objections to the House in which it shall have originated, who shall enter the objections at large on their journal, and proceed to reconsider it. If after such reconsideration two-thirds of that House shall agree to pass the bill, it shall be sent together with the objections, to the other House, by which it shall likewise be reconsidered, and if approved by two-thirds of that House, it shall become a law. But in all such cases the votes of both Houses shall be determined by yeas and nays, and the names of the persons voting for and against the bill shall be entered on the journal of each House respectively. If any bill shall not

be returned by the President within ten days (Sundays excepted) after it shall have been presented to him, the same shall be a law, in like manner as if he had signed it, unless the Congress by their adjournment prevent its return in which case it shall not be a law.

(3) Every order, resolution, of vote, to which the concurrence of the Senate and House of Representatives may be necessary (except on a question of adjournment) shall be presented to the President of the United States; and before the same shall take effect, shall be approved by him, or being disapproved by him, shall be repassed by two-thirds of the Senate and House of Representatives, according to the rules and limitations prescribed in the case of a bill.

Section 8. (1) The Congress shall have the power to lay and collect taxes, duties, imposts and excises, to pay the debts and provide for the common defense and general welfare of the United States; but all duties, imposts and excises shall be uniform throughout the United States;

(2) To borrow money on the credit of the United States;

(3) To regulate commerce with foreign nations, and among the several states, and with the Indian Tribes;

(4) To establish an uniform Rule of Naturalization, and uniform laws on the subject of bankruptcies throughout the United States;

(5) To coin money, regulate the value thereof, and of foreign coin, and fix the standard of weights and measures;

(6) To provide for the punishment of counterfeiting the securities and current coin of the United States;

(7) To establish Post Offices and Post Roads;

(8) To promote the progress of science and useful arts, by securing for limited times to authors and inventors the exclusive right to their respective writings and discoveries;

(9) To constitute tribunals inferior to the Supreme Court;

(10) To define and punish piracies and felonies committed on the high seas, and offenses against the Law of Nations;

(11) To declare war, grant Letters of Marque and Reprisal, and make rules concerning captures on land and water;

(12) To raise and support armies, but no appropriation of money to that use shall be for a longer term than two years;

(13) To provide and maintain a Navy;

(14) To make rules for the government and regulation of the land and naval forces;

(15) To provide for calling forth the Militia to execute the laws of the Union, suppress insurrections and repel invasions;

(16) To provide for organizing, arming, and disciplining, the Militia, and for governing such part of them as may be employed in the service of the United States, reserving to the states respectively, the appointment of the Officers,

and the authority of training the Militia according to the discipline prescribed by Congress;

(17) To exercise exclusive legislation in all cases whatsoever, over such district (not exceeding ten miles square) as may, by cession of particular states, and the acceptance of Congress, become the Seat of the Government of the United States, and to exercise like authority over all places purchased by the consent of the legislature of the state in which the same shall be, for the erection of forts, magazines, arsenals, dockyards, and other needful buildings; and

(18) To make all laws which shall be necessary and proper for carrying into execution the foregoing powers, and all other powers vested by this Constitution in the Government of the United States, or in any Department or Officer thereof.

Section 9. (1) The migration or importation of such persons as any of the states now existing shall think proper to admit, shall not be prohibited by the Congress prior to the year one thousand eight hundred and eight, but a tax or duty may be imposed on such importation, not exceeding ten dollars for each person.

(2) The privilege of the Writ of Habeas Corpus shall not be suspended, unless when in cases of rebellion or invasion the public safety may require it.

(3) No Bill of Attainder or ex post facto law shall be passed.

(4) No capitation, or other direct, tax shall be laid, unless in proportion to the Census or enumeration herein before directed to be taken.

(5) No tax or duty shall be laid on articles exported from any state.

(6) No preference shall be given by any regulation of commerce or revenue to the ports of one state over those of another: nor shall vessels bound to, or from, one state be obliged to enter, clear, or pay duties in another.

(7) No money shall be drawn from the Treasury, but in consequence of appropriations made by law; and a regular statement and account of the receipts and expenditures of all public money shall be published from time to time.

(8) No title of nobility shall be granted by the United States: and no person holding any office of profit or trust under them, shall, without the consent of the Congress, accept of any present, emolument, office, or title, of any kind whatever, from any King, Prince, or foreign State.

Section 10. (1) No state shall enter into any treaty, alliance, or confederation; grant Letter of Marque and Reprisal; coin money; emit bills of credit; make any thing but gold and silver coin a tender in payment of debts; pass any Bill of Attainder, ex post facto law, or law impairing the obligation of contracts, or grant any title of nobility.

(2) No state shall, without the consent of the Congress, lay any imposts or duties on imports or exports, except what may be absolutely necessary for executing its inspection laws: and the net produce of all duties and imposts, laid by any state on imports or exports, shall be for the use of

the Treasury of the United States; and all such laws shall be subject to the revision and control of the Congress.

(3) No state shall, without the consent of Congress, lay any duty of tonnage, keep troops, or ships of war in time of peace, enter into any agreement or compact with another state, or with a foreign power, or engage in war, unless actually invaded, or in such imminent danger as will not admit of delay.

ARTICLE II

Section 1. (1) The executive power shall be vested in a President of the United States of America. He shall hold his office during the term of four years, and, together with the Vice President, chosen for the same term, be elected, as follows:

(2) Each state shall appoint, in such manner as the legislature thereof may direct, a number of electors, equal to the whole number of Senators and Representatives to which the state may be entitled in the Congress; but no Senator or Representative, or person holding an office of trust or profit under the United States, shall be appointed an Elector.

(3) The Electors shall meet in their respective states, and vote by ballot for two persons, of whom one at least shall not be an inhabitant of the same state with themselves. And they shall make a list of all the persons voted for, and of the number of votes for each; which list they shall sign and certify, and transmit sealed to the Seat of the Government of the United States, directed to the President of the Senate. The President of the Senate shall, in the presence of the Senate and House of Representatives,

open all the certificates, and the votes shall then be counted. The person having the greatest number of votes shall be the President, if such number be a majority of the whole number of Electors appointed; and if there be more than one who have such majority, and have an equal number of votes, then the House of Representatives shall immediately choose by ballot one of them for President; and if no person have a majority, then from the five highest on the list the said House shall in like manner choose the President. But in choosing the President, the votes shall be taken by states the representation from each state having one vote; a quorum for this purpose shall consist of a member or members from two-thirds of the states, and a majority of all the states shall be necessary to a choice. In every case, after the choice of the President, the person having the greater number of votes of the Electors shall be the Vice President. But if there should remain two or more who have equal votes, the Senate shall choose from them by ballot the Vice President.

(4) The Congress may determine the time of choosing the Electors, and the day on which they shall give their votes; which day shall be the same throughout the United States.

(5) No person except a natural born citizen, or a citizen of the United States, at the time of the adoption of this Constitution, shall be eligible to the Office of President; neither shall any person be eligible to that Office who shall not have attained to the age of thirty-five years, and been fourteen years a resident within the United States.

(6) In case of the removal of the President from Office, or of his death, resignation or inability to discharge the powers and duties of the said Office, the same shall devolve on the Vice President, and the Congress may by law

provide for the case of removal, death, resignation, or inability, both of the President and Vice President, declaring what Officer shall then act as President, and such Officer shall act accordingly, until the disability be removed, or a President shall be elected.

(7) The President shall, at stated times, receive for his services, a compensation, which shall neither be increased nor diminished during the period for which he shall have been elected, and he shall not receive within that period any other emolument from the United States, or any of them.

(8) Before he enter on the execution of his Office, he shall take the following Oath or Affirmation: "I do solemnly swear (or affirm) that I will faithfully execute the Office of President of the United States, and will to the best of my ability, preserve, protect and defend the Constitution of the United States."

Section 2. (1) The President shall be Commander in Chief of the Army and Navy of the United States, and of the militia of the several states, when called into the actual service of the United States; he may require the opinion, in writing, of the principal Officer in each of the Executive Departments, upon any subject relating to the duties of their respective Offices, and he shall have power to grant reprieves and pardons for offenses against the United States, except in cases of impeachment.

(2) He shall have power, by and with the advice and consent of the Senate to make treaties, provided two-thirds of the Senators present concur; and he shall nominate, and by and with the advice and consent of the Senate, shall appoint Ambassadors, other public Ministers and Consuls,

Judges of the supreme Court, and all other Officers of the United States, whose appointments are not herein otherwise provided for, and which shall be established by law; but the Congress may by law vest the appointment of such inferior Officers, as they think proper, in the President alone, in the courts of law, or in the Heads of Departments.

(3) The President shall have power to fill up all vacancies that may happen during the recess of the Senate, by granting commissions which shall expire at the end of their next Session.

Section 3. He shall from time to time give to the Congress information of the State of the Union, and recommend to their consideration such measures as he shall judge necessary and expedient; he may, on extraordinary occasions, convene both Houses, or either of them, and in case of disagreement between them, with respect to the time of adjournment, he may adjourn them to such time as he shall think proper; he shall receive Ambassadors and other public Ministers; he shall take care that the laws be faithfully executed, and shall commission all the Officers of the United States.

Section 4. The President, Vice President and all civil Officers of the United States, shall be removed from office on impeachment for, and conviction of, treason, bribery, or other high crimes and misdemeanors.

ARTICLE III

Section 1. The judicial power of the United States, shall be vested in one supreme Court, and in such inferior courts as the Congress may from time to time ordain and establish. The Judges, both of the supreme and inferior courts, shall hold their Offices during good behaviour, and shall, at stated times, receive for their services a compensation, which shall not be diminished during their continuance in office.

Section 2. (1) The judicial power shall extend to all cases, in law and equity, arising under this Constitution, the laws of the United States, and treaties made, or which shall be made, under their authority; to all cases affecting Ambassadors, other public Ministers and Consuls; to all cases of admiralty and maritime jurisdiction; to controversies to which the United States shall be a party; to controversies between two or more states; between a state and citizens of another state; between citizens of different states; between citizens of the same state claiming lands under the grants of different states, and between a state, or the citizens thereof, and foreign states, citizens or subjects.

(2) In all cases affecting Ambassadors, other public Ministers and Consuls, and those in which a state shall be a party, the supreme Court shall have original jurisdiction. In all the other cases before mentioned, the supreme Court shall have appellate jurisdiction, both as to law and fact, with such exceptions, and under such regulations as the Congress shall make.

(3) The trial of all crimes, except in cases of impeachment, shall be by jury; and such trial shall be held in the state where the said crimes shall have been committed; but when not committed within any state, the trial shall be at such place or places as the Congress may by law have directed.

Section 3. (1) Treason against the United States, shall consist only in levying war against them, or, in adhering to their enemies, giving them aid and comfort. No person shall be convicted of treason unless on the testimony of two witnesses to the same overt act, or on confession in open Court.

(2) The Congress shall have power to declare the punishment of treason, but no Attainder of Treason shall work corruption of blood, or forfeiture except during the life of the person attainted.

ARTICLE IV

Section 1. Full faith and credit shall be given in each state to the public acts, records, and judicial proceedings of every other state. And the Congress may by general laws prescribe the manner in which such acts, records and proceedings shall be proved, and the effect thereof.

Section 2. (1) The citizens of each state shall be entitled to all privileges and immunities of citizens in the several states.

(2) A person charged in any state with treason, felony, or other crime, who shall flee from justice, and be found in another state, shall on demand of the executive authority of the state from which he fled, be delivered up, to be removed to the state having jurisdiction of the crime.

(3) No person held to service or labour in one state, under the laws thereof, escaping into another, shall, in consequence of any law or regulation therein, be discharged from such service or labour, but shall be delivered up on

claim of the party to whom such service or labour may be due.

Section 3. (1) New states may be admitted by the Congress into this Union; but no new state shall be formed or erected within the jurisdiction of any other state; nor any state be formed by the junction of two or more states, or parts of states, without the consent of the legislatures of the states concerned as well as of the Congress.

(2) The Congress shall have power to dispose of and make all needful rules and regulations respecting the territory or other property belonging to the United States; and nothing in this Constitution shall be so construed as to prejudice any claims of the United States, or of any particular state.

Section 4. The United States shall guarantee to every state in this Union a Republican form of government, and shall protect each of them against invasion; and on application of the Legislature, or of the Executive (when the Legislature cannot be convened) against domestic violence.

ARTICLE V

The Congress, whenever two-thirds of both Houses shall deem it necessary, shall propose amendments to this Constitution, or, on the application of the Legislatures of two-thirds of the several states, shall call a convention for proposing amendments, which, in either case, shall be valid to all intents and purposes, as part of this constitution, when ratified by the Legislatures of three-fourths of the several states, or by conventions in three-fourths thereof, as the one or the other mode of ratification may be proposed by the Congress; provided that no amendment which may be made prior to the year one thousand eight hundred and eight shall in any manner affect the first and fourth clauses in the Ninth Section of the first Article; and that no state, without its consent, shall be deprived of its equal suffrage in the Senate.

ARTICLE VI

(1) All debts contracted and engagements entered into, before the adoption of this Constitution shall be as valid against the United States under this Constitution, as under the Confederation.

(2) This Constitution, and the laws of the United States which shall be made in pursuance thereof; and all treaties made, or which shall be made, under the authority of the United States, shall be the supreme law of the land; and the Judges in every state shall be bound thereby, any thing in the Constitution or laws of any state to the contrary notwithstanding.

(3) The Senators and Representatives before mentioned, and the Members of the several State Legislatures, and all executive and judicial Officers, both of the United States and of the several states, shall be bound by oath or affirmation, to support this Constitution; but no religious test shall ever be required as a qualification to any Office or public trust under the United States.

ARTICLE VII

The ratification of the Conventions of nine states shall be sufficient for the establishment of this Constitution between the states so ratifying the same.

AMENDMENT I (1791)

Congress shall make no law respecting an establishment of religion, or prohibiting the free exercise thereof; or abridging the freedom of speech, or of the press; or the right of the people peaceably to assemble, and to petition the Government for a redress of grievances.

AMENDMENT II (1791)

A well regulated Militia, being necessary to the security of a free State, the right of the people to keep and bear arms, shall not be infringed.

AMENDMENT III (1791)

No soldier shall, in time of peace be quartered in any house, without the consent of the owner, nor in time of war, but in a manner to be prescribed by law.

AMENDMENT IV (1791)

The right of the people to be secure in their persons, houses, papers, and effects, against unreasonable searches and seizures, shall not be violated, and no warrants shall issue, but upon probable cause, supported by oath or affirmation, and particularly describing the place to be searched, and the persons or things to be seized.

AMENDMENT V (1791)

No person shall be held to answer for a capital, or otherwise infamous crime, unless on a presentment or indictment of a Grand Jury, except in cases arising in the land or naval forces, or in the Militia, when in actual service in time of war or public danger; nor shall any person be subject for the same offense to be twice put in jeopardy of life or limb; nor shall be compelled in any criminal case to be a witness against himself, nor be deprived of life, liberty, or property, without due process of law; nor shall private property be taken for public use, without just compensation.

AMENDMENT VI (1791)

In all criminal prosecutions, the accused shall enjoy the right to a speedy and public trial, by an impartial jury of the state and district wherein the crime shall have been committed, which district shall have been previously ascertained by law, and to be informed of the nature and cause of the accusation; to be confronted with the witnesses against him; to have compulsory process for obtaining witnesses in his favor, and to have the assistance of counsel for his defense.

AMENDMENT VII (1791)

In suits at common law, where the value in controversy shall exceed twenty dollars, the right of trial by jury shall be preserved, and no fact tried by jury, shall be otherwise re-examined in any Court of the United States, than according to the rules of the common law.

AMENDMENT VIII (1791)

Excessive bail shall not be required, nor excessive fines imposed, nor cruel and unusual punishments inflicted.

AMENDMENT IX (1791)

The enumeration in the Constitution, of certain rights, shall not be construed to deny or disparage others retained by the people.

AMENDMENT X (1791)

The powers not delegated to the United States by the Constitution, nor prohibited by it to the States, are reserved to the States respectively, or to the people.

AMENDMENT XI (1798)

The judicial power of the United States shall not be construed to extend to any suit in law or equity, commenced or prosecuted against one of the United States by citizens of another state, or by citizens or subjects of any foreign state.

AMENDMENT XII (1804)

The Electors shall meet in their respective states and vote by ballot for President and Vice-President, one of whom, at least, shall not be an inhabitant of the same state with themselves; they shall name in their ballots the person voted for as President, and in distinct ballots the person voted for as Vice-President, and they shall make distinct lists of all persons voted for as President, and of all persons voted for as Vice-President, and of the number of votes for each, which lists they shall sign and certify, and transmit sealed to the seat of the government of the United States, directed to the President of the Senate; the President of the Senate shall, in the presence of the Senate and House of Representatives, open all the certificates and the votes shall then be counted; the person having the greatest number of votes for President, shall be the President, if such number be a majority of the persons having the highest numbers not exceeding three on the list of those voted for as President, the House of Representatives shall choose immediately, by ballot, the President. But in choosing the President, the votes shall be taken by states, the representation from each state having one vote; a quorum for this purpose shall consist of a member or members from two-thirds of the states, and a majority of all the states shall be necessary to a choice. And if the House of Representatives shall not choose a President whenever the right of choice shall devolve upon them before the fourth day of March next following, then the Vice-President shall act as President, as in the case of the death or other constitutional disability of the President. The person having the greatest number of votes as Vice-President, shall be the Vice-President, if such number be a majority of the whole number of Electors appointed, and if no person have a majority, then from the two highest numbers on the list, the Senate shall choose the Vice-President; a quorum for the purpose shall consist of two-thirds of the whole number of Senators, and a majority of the whole number shall be necessary to a choice. But no person constitutionally ineligible to the office of President shall be eligible to that of Vice-President of the United States.

AMENDMENT XIII (1865)

Section 1. Neither slavery nor involuntary servitude, except as a punishment for crime whereof the party shall have been duly convicted, shall exist within the United States, or any place subject to their jurisdiction.

Section 2. Congress shall have power to enforce this article by appropriate legislation.

AMENDMENT XIV (1868)

Section 1. All persons born or naturalized in the United States, and subject to the jurisdiction thereof, are citizens of the United States and of the state wherein they reside. No state shall make or enforce any law which shall abridge the privileges or immunities of citizens of the United States; nor shall any state deprive any person of life, liberty, or property, without due process of law; nor deny to any person within its jurisdiction the equal protection of the laws.

Section 2. Representatives shall be apportioned among the several states according to their respective numbers, counting the whole number of persons in each State excluding Indians not taxed. But when the right to vote at any election for the choice of electors for President and Vice President of the United States, Representatives in Congress, the Executive and Judicial officers of a state, or the members of the Legislature thereof, is denied to any of the male inhabitants of such state, being twenty-one years of age, and citizens of the United States, or in any way abridged, except for participation in rebellion, or other crime, the basis of representation therein shall be reduced in the proportion which the number of such male citizens shall bear to the whole number of male citizens twenty-one years of age in such state.

Section 3. No person shall be a Senator or Representative in Congress, or elector of President and Vice President, or hold any office, civil or military, under the United States, or under any state, who having previously taken an oath, as a member of Congress, or as an officer of the United States, or as a member of any state legislature, or as an executive or judicial officer of any state, to support the Constitution of the United States, shall have engaged in insurrection or rebellion against the same, or given aid or comfort to the enemies thereof. But Congress may by a vote of two-thirds of each House, remove such disability.

Section 4. The validity of the public debt of the United States, authorized by law, including debts incurred for payment of pensions and bounties for services in suppressing insurrection or rebellion, shall not be questioned. But neither the United States nor any state shall assume or pay any debt or obligation incurred in aid of insurrection or rebellion against the United States, or any claim for the loss or emancipation of any slave; but all such debts, obligations and claims shall be held illegal and void.

Section 5. The Congress shall have power to enforce, by appropriate legislation, the provisions of this article.

AMENDMENT XV (1870)

Section 1. The right of citizens of the United States to vote shall not be denied or abridged by the United States or by any state on account of race, color, or previous condition of servitude.

Section 2. The Congress shall have power to enforce this article by appropriate legislation.

AMENDMENT XVI (1913)

The Congress shall have power to lay and collect taxes on income, from whatever source derived, without apportionment among the several states, and without regard to any census or enumeration.

AMENDMENT XVII (1913)

(1) The Senate of the United States shall be composed of two Senators from each state, elected by the people thereof, for six years; and each Senator shall have one vote. The electors in each State shall have the qualifications requisite for electors of the most numerous branch of the state legislatures.

(2) When vacancies happen in the representation of any state in the Senate, the executive authority of such state shall issue writs of election to fill such vacancies: *provided,* that the legislature of any state may empower the executive thereof to make temporary appointments until the people fill the vacancies by election as the legislature may direct.

(3) This amendment shall not be so construed as to affect the election or term of any Senator chosen before it becomes valid as part of the Constitution.

AMENDMENT XVIII (1919)

Section 1. After one year from the ratification of this article the manufacture, sale, or transportation of intoxicating liquors within, the importation thereof into, or the exportation thereof from the United States and all territory subject to the jurisdiction thereof for beverage purposes is hereby prohibited.

Section 2. The Congress and the several states shall have concurrent power to enforce this article by appropriate legislation.

Section 3. This article shall be inoperative unless it shall have been ratified as an amendment to the Constitution by the legislatures of the several states, as provided in the Constitution, within seven years from the date of the submission hereof to the states by the Congress.

AMENDMENT XIX (1920)

(1) The right of citizens of the United States to vote shall not be denied or abridged by the United States or by any state on account of sex.

(2) Congress shall have power to enforce this article by appropriate legislation.

AMENDMENT XX (1933)

Section 1. The terms of the President and Vice President shall end at noon on the 20th day of January, and the terms of Senators and Representatives at noon on the 3d day of January, of the years in which such terms would have ended if this article had not been ratified; and the terms of their successors shall then begin.

Section 2. The Congress shall assemble at least once in every year, and such meeting shall begin at noon on the 3d day of January, unless they shall by law appoint a different day.

Section 3. If, at the time fixed for the beginning of the term of the President, the President elect shall have died, the Vice President elect shall become President. If the President shall not have been chosen before the time fixed for the beginning of his term, or if the President elect shall have failed to qualify, then the Vice President elect shall act as President until a President shall have qualified; and the Congress may by law provide for the case wherein neither a President elect nor a Vice President elect shall have qualified, declaring who shall then act as President, or the manner in which one who is to act shall be selected, and such person shall act accordingly until a President or Vice President shall have qualified.

Section 4. The Congress may by law provide for the case of the death of any of the persons from whom the House of Representatives may choose a President whenever the right of choice shall have devolved upon them, and for the case of the death of any of the persons from whom the Senate may choose a Vice President whenever the right of choice shall have devolved upon them.

Section 5. Sections 1 and 2 shall take effect on the 15th day of October following the ratification of this article.

Section 6. This article shall be inoperative unless it shall have been ratified as an amendment to the Constitution by the legislatures of three-fourths of the several states within seven years from the date of its submission.

AMENDMENT XXI (1933)

Section 1. The eighteenth article of amendment to the Constitution of the United States is hereby repealed.

Section 2. The transportation or importation into any state, territory, or possession of the United States for delivery or use therein of intoxicating liquors, in violation of the laws thereof, is hereby prohibited.

Section 3. This article shall be inoperative unless it shall have been ratified as an amendment to the Constitution by conventions in the several states, as provided in the Constitution, within seven years from the date of the submission hereof to the states by the Congress.

AMENDMENT XXII (1951)

Section 1. No person shall be elected to the office of the President more than twice, and no person who has held the office of President, or acted as President, for more than two years of a term to which some other person was elected President shall be elected to the office of President more than once. But this Article shall not apply to any person holding the office of President when this Article was proposed by the Congress, and shall not prevent any person who may be holding the office of President, or acting as President, during the term within which this Article becomes operative from holding the office of President or acting as President during the remainder of such term.

Section 2. This article shall be inoperative unless it shall have been ratified as an amendment to the Constitution by the legislatures of three-fourths of the several states within seven years from the date of its submission to the states by the Congress.

AMENDMENT XXIII (1961)

Section 1. The District constituting the seat of Government of the United States shall appoint in such manner as the Congress may direct:

A number of electors of President and Vice President equal to the whole number of Senators and Representatives in Congress to which the District would be entitled if it were a state, but in no event more than the least populous state; they shall be in addition to those appointed by the states, but they shall be considered, for the purposes of the election of President and Vice President, to be electors appointed by a state; and they shall meet in the District and perform such duties as provided by the twelfth article of amendment.

Section 2. The Congress shall have power to enforce this article by appropriate legislation.

AMENDMENT XXIV (1964)

Section 1. The right of citizens of the United States to vote in any primary or other election for President or Vice President, for electors for President or Vice President, or for Senator or Representative in Congress, shall not be denied or abridged by the United States, or any state by reason of failure to pay any poll tax or other tax.

Section 2. The Congress shall have power to enforce this article by appropriate legislation.

AMENDMENT XXV (1967)

Section 1. In case of the removal of the President from office or of his death or resignation, the Vice President shall become President.

Section 2. Whenever there is a vacancy in the office of the Vice President, the President shall nominate a Vice President who shall take office upon confirmation by a majority vote of both Houses of Congress.

Section 3. Whenever the President transmits to the President pro tempore of the Senate and the Speaker of the House of Representatives his written declaration that he is unable to discharge the powers and duties of his office, and until he transmits to them a written declaration to the contrary, such powers and duties shall be discharged by the Vice President as Acting President.

Section 4. Whenever the Vice President and a majority of either the principal officers of the executive departments or of such other body as Congress may by law provide, transmit to the President pro tempore of the Senate and the Speaker of the House of Representatives their written declaration that the President is unable to discharge the powers and duties of his office, the Vice President shall immediately assume the powers and duties of the office as Acting President.

Thereafter, when the President transmits to the President pro tempore of the Senate and the Speaker of the House of Representatives his written declaration that no inability exists, he shall resume the powers and duties of his office unless the Vice President and a majority of either the principal officers of the executive department or of such other body as Congress may by law provide, transmit within four days to the President pro tempore of the Senate and the Speaker of the House of Representatives their written declaration that the President is unable to discharge the powers and duties of his office. Thereupon Congress shall decide the issue, assembling within forty-eight hours for that purpose if not in session. If the Congress, within twenty-one days after receipt of the latter written declaration, or, if Congress is not in session, within twenty-one days after Congress is required to assemble, determines by two-thirds vote of both Houses that the President is unable to discharge the power and duties of his office, the Vice President shall continue to discharge the same as Acting President; otherwise, the President shall resume the powers and duties of his office.

AMENDMENT XXVI (1971)

Section 1. The right of citizens of the United States, who are eighteen years of age or older, to vote shall not be denied or abridged by the United States or by any state on account of age.

Section 2. The Congress shall have power to enforce this article by appropriate legislation.

AMENDMENT XXVII (1992)

No law, varying the compensation for the services of the Senators and Representatives, shall take effect, until an election of Representatives shall have intervened.

BIBLIOGRAPHY

Malicious and Scandalous Newspapers

Clurman, Richard M. *Beyond Malice: The Media's Years of Reckoning.* New Brunswick, NJ: Transaction, 1988.

Cranberg, Gilbert. *Malice in Wonderland: Intrusion in the Newsroom.* Iowa City, IA: University of Iowa, 1992.

Worton, Stanley N. *Freedom of Speech and Press.* Rochelle Park, NJ: Hayden Book Co., 1975.

The Libel of Public Officials

Hopkins, W.W. *Actual Malice: Twenty-Five Years After Times v. Sullivan.* New York, NY: Praeger, 1989.

Lawhorne, Clifton O. *Defamation and Public Officials: The Evolving Law of Libel.* Carbondale, IL: Southern Illinois University Press, 1971.

Lewis, Anthony. *Make No Law: The Sullivan Case and The First Amendment.* New York, NY: Random House, 1991.

New York Times v. Sullivan: The Next Twenty Years. New York, NY: Practising Law Institute, 1984.

The Pentagon Papers

Ungar, Sanford J. *The Papers and The Papers: An Account of the Legal and Political Battle Over the Pentagon Papers.* New York, NY: Dutton, 1979.

The Rape Shield Law

Cook, Virginia G. *Shield Laws: A Report on Freedom of the Press, Protection of News Sources, and the Obligation to Testify.* Lexington, KY: Council of State Governments, 1973.

The Infliction of Emotional Distress

Nimmer, Melville B., "The Meaning of Symbolic Speech to the First Amendment," *UCLA Law Review* 21: 29-62.

Post, Robert C., "The Constitutional Concept of Public Discourse: Outrageous Opinion, Democratic Deliberation, and Hustler Magazine v. Falwell," *Harvard Law Review*, Vol. 103, No. 3 (Jan. 1990).

Smolla, Rodney A., *Jerry Falwell v. Larry Flynt: The First Amendment on Trial*, New York, NY: St. Martin's Press, 1988.

The Right to Reply

The Trial of the First Amendment: Miami Herald v. Tornillo. Columbia, MO: Freedom of Information Center, 1975.

Protecting Confidential News Sources

Simons, Howard, and Joseph A. Califano. *The Media and the Law.* New York, NY: Praeger, 1976.

The Fairness Doctrine

Donahue, Hugh C. *The Battle to Control Broadcast News: Who Owns the First Amendment?* Cambridge, MA: MIT Press, 1989.

Simmons, Steven J. *The Fairness Doctrine and the Media.* Berkeley, CA: University of California Press, 1978.

Pretrial Publicity

Winters, Glenn R., Editor. *Fair Trial - Free Press.* Chicago, IL: American Judicature Society, 1971.

The Juvenile Shield Law

Humes, Edward. *No Matter How Loud I Shout: A Year in the Life of Juvenile Court.* New York, NY: Simon & Schuster, 1996.

Reinharz, Peter. *Killer Kids, Bad Law: Tales of the Juvenile Court System.* New York, NY: Barricade Books, 1996.

Gagging the Press

Gora, Joel M. *The Rights of Reporters: The Basic ACLU Guide to a Reporter's Rights.* New York, NY: Sunrise Books, 1974.

Kelly, Sean. *Access Denied: The Politics of Press Censorship.* Beverly Hills, CA: Sage Publications, 1978.

Excluding the Press

Hemmer, Joseph J. *Journalistic Freedom.* Metuchen, NJ: Scarecrow Press, 1980.

Nelson, Harold L., and Dwight L. Teeter, Jr. *Law of Mass Communications: Freedom and Control of Print and Broadcast Media.* Mineola, NY: Foundation Press, 1969.

Pickerell, Albert G., and Michel Lipman. *The Courts and the News Media*. Berkeley, CA: Conference of California Judges, 1974.

Schmidt, Benno C. *Freedom of the Press Vs. Public Access*. New York, NY: Praeger, 1976.

Searches and Seizures in Newsrooms

Trager, Robert, and Donna L. Dickerson. *College Student Press Law*. Terre Haute, IN: National Council of College Publications Advisors, 1976.

X-Rated Cable Broadcasts

Carter, T. Barton, Marc A. Franklin, and Jay B. Wright. *The First Amendment and the Fifth Estate: Regulation of Electronic Mass Media*. Mineola, NY: Foundation Press, 1986.

The First Amendment and Freedom of the Press

Barron, Jerome A. *Freedom of the Press for Whom? The Right of Access to Mass Media*. Bloomington, IN: Indiana University Press, 1973.

Barron, Jerome A., and C. Thomas Dienes. *Handbook of Free Speech and Free Press.* Boston, MA: Little, Brown, 1979.

Chenery, William L. *Freedom of the Press.* Westport, CT: Greenwood Press, 1977.

Clark, David G., and Earl R. Hutchison. *Mass Media and the Law: Freedom and Restraint.* New York, NY: Wiley-Interscience, 1970.

Cullen, Maurice R. *Mass Media and the First Amendment: An Introduction to the Issues, Problems, and Practices.* Dubuque, IA: W.C. Brown Co., 1981.

Devol, Kenneth S. *Mass Media and the Supreme Court: The Legacy of the Warren Years.* New York, NY: Hastings House, 1971.

Francois, William E. *Mass Media Law and Regulation.* Ames, IA: Iowa State University Press, 1990.

Hehenberg, John. *Free Press/Free People: The Best Cause.* New York, NY: Columbia University Press, 1971.

Hemmer, Joseph J. *The Supreme Court and the First Amendment.* New York, NY: Praeger, 1986.

Holsinger, Ralph L. *Media Law.* New York, NY: Random House, 1987.

Lively, Donald E. *Modern Communications Law.* New York, NY: Praeger, 1991.

Lofton, John. *The Press as Guardian of the First Amendment.* Columbia, SC: University of South Carolina Press, 1980.

McCoy, Ralph E. *Freedom of the Press: An Annotated Bibliography.* Carbondale, IL: Southern Illinois University Press, 1968.

Nelson, Harold L. *Freedom of the Press from Hamilton to the Warren Court.* Indianapolis, IN: Bobbs-Merrill, 1967.

Pember, Don R. *Mass Media Law.* Dubuque, IA: W.C. Brown, 1990.

Rogers, Donald J. *Press Versus Government: Constitutional Issues.* New York, NY: J. Messner, 1986.

Schwartz, Bernard. *Freedom of the Press.* New York, NY: Facts on File, 1992.

Seldes, George. *Freedom of the Press.* New York, NY: Da Capo Press, 1971.

Siebert, Fred S. *The Rights and Privileges of the Press.* Westport, CT: Greenwood Press, 1934.

Smolla, Rodney A. *Suing the Press.* New York, NY: Oxford University Press, 1986.

Spencer, Dale R. *Law for the Newsman.* Columbia, MO: Lucas Brothers, 1971.

Steigleman, Walter A. *The Newspaperman and the Law.* Westport, CT: Greenwood Press, 1971.

Stein, Meyer L. *Shaping the News: How the Media Function in Today's World.* New York, NY: Washington Square Press, 1974.

Zelezny, John D. *Communications Law: Liberties, Restraints, and the Modern Media.* Belmont, CA: Wadsworth Publishing Co., 1993.

Zerman, Melvyn B. *Taking on the Press: Constitutional Rights in Conflict.* New York, NY: Crowell, 1986.

THE SUPREME COURT

Agresto, John. *The Supreme Court and Constitutional Democracy.* Ithaca, NY: Cornell University Press, 1984.

Cox, Archibald. *The Court and the Constitution.* New York, NY: Houghton-Mifflin, 1988.

Dumbauld, Edward. *The Bill of Rights and What It Means Today.* New York, NY: Greenwood Press, 1979.

Goode, Stephen. *The Controversial Court: Supreme Court Influences on American Life.* New York, NY: Messner, 1982.

Lawson, Don. *Landmark Supreme Court Cases.* Hillside: Enslow Publishers, Inc. 1987.

Rehnquist, William H. *The Supreme Court: How It Was, How It Is.* New York, NY: Morrow, 1987.

Woodward, Bob, and Scott Armstrong. *The Brethren: Inside the Supreme Court.* New York, NY: Simon & Schuster, 1979.

Yudof, Mark. *When Government Speaks: Politics, Law, and Government Expression in America.* Berkeley, CA: University of California Press, 1983.

Index

Congress shall make no law respecting an establishment of religion or prohibiting the free exercise thereof.

FREEDOM OF RELIGION DECISIONS OF THE UNITED STATES SUPREME COURT

This volume of the **First Amendment Decisions Series** provides the actual legal text of historic **Freedom of Religion Decisions of The United States Supreme Court**, edited into plain, non-legal English. **Freedom of Religion Decisions** includes such significant cases as: the school prayer decision, teaching Darwin's "non-religion" theory of evolution, public preaching and street proselytizing, the Christmas creche controversy, and tax exemptions for churches.

Congress shall make no law abridging the freedom of speech.

FREEDOM OF SPEECH DECISIONS OF THE UNITED STATES SUPREME COURT

This volume of the **First Amendment Decisions Series** presents the actual text of thirteen historic **Freedom of Speech Decisions of The United States Supreme Court**, edited into plain non-legal English. **Freedom of Speech Decisions of The United States Supreme Court** includes such significant cases as: "Shouting 'Fire!' in a Crowded Theater"; fighting words; violent speech; the cross burning case; schoolhouse speech; the right to read; the flag burning case; civil rights demonstrations; abortion clinic picketing; and draft card burning.

EXCELLENT BOOKS ORDER FORM
(Please xerox this form so it will be available to other readers.)

Please send

Copy(ies)
_____ of FREEDOM OF THE PRESS DECISIONS @ $16.95 each
_____ of FREEDOM OF RELIGION DECISIONS @ $16.95 each
_____ of FREEDOM OF SPEECH DECISIONS @ $16.95 each
_____ of THE MURDER REFERENCE @ $16.95 each
_____ of THE RAPE REFERENCE @ $16.95 each
_____ of LANDMARK DECISIONS @ $16.95 each
_____ of LANDMARK DECISIONS II @ $16.95 each
_____ of LANDMARK DECISIONS III @ $16.95 each
_____ of LANDMARK DECISIONS IV @ $16.95 each
_____ of LANDMARK DECISIONS V @ $16.95 each
_____ of ABORTION DECISIONS: THE 1970's @ $16.95 each
_____ of ABORTION DECISIONS: THE 1980's @ $16.95 each
_____ of ABORTION DECISIONS: THE 1990's @ $16.95 each
_____ of CIVIL RIGHTS DECISIONS: 19th CENTURY @ $16.95 ea.
_____ of CIVIL RIGHTS DECISIONS: 20th CENTURY @ $16.95 ea.
_____ of THE ADA HANDBOOK @ $16.95 each

Name: _____

Address: _____

City: _____ **State:** _____ **Zip:** _____

Add $1 per book for shipping and handling
California residents add sales tax

OUR GUARANTEE: Any Excellent Book may be returned at any time for any reason and a full refund will be made.

Mail your check or money order to: Excellent Books, Post Office Box 927105, San Diego, California 92192-7105 or call/fax (619) 598-5069